The Excel
VBA User Form Conundrum Solved
The slim version with more filling!

Richard's Journals

TM

Richard Brooks

www.richardsjournals.com

Hello.
This book is for you!

Richard's
Journals

TM

Designed to help answer the
most often asked questions for
this type of project. We deliver
a step-by-step process with a
simple and easy to follow
straightforward approach.

Credits

The Development Staff at Richard's Journals created and designed all the material referenced in this book and if included also on the accompanying files or CD.

Trademarks

Richard's Journals, "The slim version with more filling!" and the logos referenced in this book are trademarks and service marks of Richard's Journals. Microsoft, Excel, Visual Basic, and Windows are either registered trademarks or trademarks of Microsoft Corporation in the United States and other countries. Also, Adobe Fireworks and Photoshop are either registered trademarks or trademarks of Adobe in the United Sates or other countries. All other product names and services referenced throughout this book are trademarks or registered trademarks of their respective company. The product names and services are used throughout this book in editorial fashion, training and for identification purposes only. No such use, or the use of any trade name, is intended to convey endorsement or other affiliation with the book and if included any related files or CD.

Warning and Disclaimer

Richard's Journals takes great care to ensure the accuracy and quality of these materials, and every effort has been made to make this book and if included, any accompanying files as complete and as accurate as possible, but no warranty of fitness is implied. The information within this book is a quick and slim condensed version so the author and publisher can keep you focused on the facts and key points. Information in this book is distributed on an "As Is" basis with no expressed or implied guarantees or promises of success. This Book is intended to be used purely for entertainment and training purposes. This book is sold with the understanding that the author and publisher are not engaged in rendering professional advice or services. If other expert assistance is required, the services of a competent certified professional should be sought.

This book expresses the author's view and opinions. The information contained in this book is provided without any express, statutory, or implied warranties. Neither the author, the publisher, nor its resellers, or distributors will be held liable nor responsible to any person or entity with respect to any loss or damages caused or alleged to be caused directly or indirectly by the instructions, errors or omissions, contained herein this book or from the use of the book, and if included CD, or files accompanying it, or by the computer software and hardware products described.

This book references links to third-party Web sites that are not under the control of the author and its publisher. Therefore they are not responsible for the content on any linked site. If you access a third-party Web site mentioned in this book, then you do so at your own risk. The author and publisher provide these links only as a convenience, and the inclusion of the link does not imply that the author or the publisher endorses or accepts any responsibility for the content on those third-party sites.

The example companies, organizations, products, domain names, e-mail addresses, logos, people, places, and events depicted herein are fictitious. No association with any real company, organization, product, domain name, e-mail address, logo, person, place, or event is intended or should be inferred and is purely coincidental.

Terms and Conditions

IMPORTANT NOTICE: This information is provided for general information purposes only and is not legal advice. Richard's Journals reserves the right, at its sole discretion, to change or modify, add or remove portions of these Terms of Use, and this policy at any time without notice. The tutorials on Richard's Journals books and website are the copyright of Richard's Journals. You may use the effects demonstrated in these tutorials in your own work – commercial or non-commercial provided the outcome of tutorials are not to be used for resale, profit or redistribution. BY USING THIS BOOK OR RICHARD'S JOURNALS SITE, YOU AGREE TO THESE TERMS OF USE; IF YOU DO NOT AGREE, PLEASE DO NOT USE THIS BOOK OR RICHARD'S JOURNALS SITE.

Richard's Journals Permissions and trademark guidelines

The following guidelines are provided for the use of certain Richard's Journals copyrighted materials, such as images, box shots, screen shots, and text; and for the use of certain trademarked materials, such as logos, marks, and icons. These materials are owned by Richard's Journals and provided under license. To use such materials, you must first agree to the following license terms:

1. The materials available for download on any Richard's Journals sites (collectively, the "Site") and within this book are subject to these license terms, as well as any specific guidelines contained therein. If you download any materials from the Site, you agree to be bound by these license terms as well as the specific guidelines related to the materials you wish to download.

2. You may not sell, alter, modify, license, sublicense, copy, or use the materials in any way other than has been specifically authorized by Richard's Journals in the Richard's Journals permissions and trademark guidelines described herein.

3. You acknowledge that Richard's Journals reserves the right to revoke the authorization to view download, and print the materials available on the Site at any time, and for any reason; and such authorization shall be deemed to be discontinued immediately upon the removal of these materials from the site.

4. You acknowledge that any rights granted to you constitute a license and not a transfer of title. You do not obtain any ownership right, title, or other interest in Richard's Journals copyrighted materials or trademarks by downloading, copying, or otherwise using these materials.

5. RICHARD'S JOURNALS SHALL NOT BE LIABLE TO YOU OR ANY OTHER PARTY FOR ANY LOSS OF REVENUE OR PROFIT OR FOR INDIRECT, INCIDENTAL, SPECIAL, CONSEQUENTIAL, OR OTHER SIMILAR DAMAGES, WHETHER BASED ON TORT (INCLUDING, WITHOUT LIMITATION, NEGLIGENCE OR STRICT LIABILITY), CONTRACT, OR OTHER LEGAL OR EQUITABLE GROUNDS EVEN IF RICHARD'S JOURNALS HAS BEEN ADVISED OR HAD REASON TO KNOW OF THE POSSIBILITY OF SUCH DAMAGES.

6. ANY MATERIALS ARE PROVIDED ON AN "AS IS BASIS, RICHARD'S JOURNALS SPECIFICALLY DISCLAIMS ALL EXPRESS, STATUTORY, OR IMPLIED WARRANTIES RELATING TO THESE MATERIALS, INCLUDING BUT NOT LIMITED TO THOSE CONCERNING MERCHANTABILITY OR FITNESS FOR A PARTICULAR PURPOSE OR NON-INFRINGEMENT OF ANY THIRD-PARTY RIGHTS REGARDING THE MATERIALS.

Save As

Excel 97 – 2004 Workbook.xls

The .xls file format is compatible with Excel 97 through Excel 2003 for Windows and Excel 98 through Excel 2004 for Mac. Saving in this format will permit you to preserve the Visual Basic Application (VBA) macro code and Excel 4.0 macro sheets needed for creating User Forms. Therefore, when creating any User Form, make sure you save your Microsoft Excel workbook in the format .xls.

A Note to the Reader

So we can get straight to the point without having to filter through too much basic discussion, we made every effort to limit unnecessary content within this book.

The assumption is the user of this book has some basic knowledge of the usage of Excel and some familiarity of Microsoft Windows operating system.

About the Author

Richard Brooks has had an extensive career with a number of Fortune 500 companies. He has worked on the business side managing various departments including Call Centers, Central Communications, Corporate PC Training, Restaurants, Theme Park Production Bakery, Security System Access, Report Development, Inventory Management, and Space Planning divisions. On the IT side, he has designed, engineered and managed the development of corporate applications.

During his employment over the years he has been tasked to streamline business processes, improve productivity, and to create a synergy between their existing applications and software products. These challenges have resulted in the production of many powerful user-friendly applications.

For this book he has drawn on his experience working with SQL, SharePoint, InfoPath, Crystal Reports, XML, HTML, CSS, .NET, SSRS, VBA, Adobe and numerous Microsoft Office products to name just a few. Each book in the series of Richard's Journals is based on his journey to produce solid applications that can be utilized for various business and personal needs.

Unlike many other books that give you broad answers to your development questions, he has decided to get straight to the point and provide a simple approach to giving clear concise direction for useful projects that can be molded to fit your specific needs. This book is for everyone. The step-by-step direction will give you the edge for your new or existing position within a company.

Author's Acknowledgements

My Wife

I want to thank my beautiful wife, Christina, who has believed in me from the day we met and strongly encouraged me to translate my notes into a book. Without her love, patience and friendship I could not have considered the possibility of moving forward in life. She has and will forever be my love, my closest friend and the center of my universe.

My Children

I am a very proud father of three wonderful sons who have been a daily inspiration in my life. Their positive outlook and laughter is infectious. They are a constant reminder of the finer things I have in my life and of how very blessed I am. Christopher, Devin and Matthew are each individually gifted artistically, intellectually and musically in their own right.

My Parents

To my mother for demonstrating how strength and courage will overcome all obstacles. Most of all, I truly appreciate how through her own actions, she taught me how to shake off the craziness in life and forge forward. To my father for enduring life's challenges with the strength I can only hope to have in my later years of life and for watching over me from the heavens above.

Table of contents

Chapter 1: User Form 101

Chapter 2: The Process

Chapter 3: Images

Chapter 4: The Basics

Chapter 5: User Form & Objects

Chapter 6: Code: Inside & Out

Chapter 7: Step-by-Step

Appendix A: Project Checklist

Appendix B: User Form Guide

Chapter 1:
User Form 101

What is a User Form?

The Data Repository

The User Form Image

Various uses of a User Form

Save As

The Power of a Professional User Form

Parts of a User Form

What is a User Form?

Microsoft Excel is a powerful spreadsheet application. Similar to a paper ledger, a spreadsheet looks like an electronic grid that consists of rows, columns and cells. Each spreadsheet consists of millions of individual cells and each one can hold up to 32, 767 characters. The individual spreadsheets within Excel are maintained within a Workbook. The total numbers of spreadsheets a workbook can contain are only limited by your computer systems memory. Therefore, allowing a user to track massive amounts of information.

Unlike Microsoft Word that serves a specific function, the spreadsheets within a Microsoft Excel workbook has many uses. College students, Engineers, Accountants, teachers, corporations, and the everyday user can greatly benefit from the applications built in features such as multiple calculations capability, relational analysis and graphing/chart functionality.

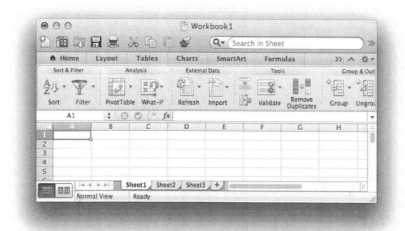

Often overlooked and less talked about is the power and strength of the macro programming language referred to as Visual Basic for Applications (VBA) that is built into each Microsoft Office product. Here in this book we will focus on the benefits of using VBA code in conjunction with a graphical user interface (GUI) referred to as a User Form. Through the creative design of a User Form, along with the backend support of VBA coding you will learn how to enhance the user's experience with Excel.

A User Form is a dialog box consisting of one or more objects. It can be designed to permit the user to capture, interact, manipulate, manage and easily navigate through the large amounts of information on a spreadsheet. Below are two different examples of a User Form. One uses the image and the other does not. Both are equally functional. But, only one is truly eye catching and professional looking.

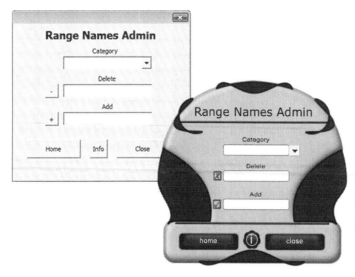

Some of the tools used to create the User Forms referenced in this book are:

- Microsoft Excel workbook

- Visual Basic Editor (VBE)

- *Graphics Editing / Desktop Publishing Software

*The Excel workbook and VBE is all that is required to create a simple basic User Form and as such additional software is not required. However, the Graphics Editing / Desktop Publishing Software is an additional tool used throughout this book to create professional looking User Forms.

The Data Repository

The Excel worksheets in a workbook act as a repository by collecting data from the User Form and allowing you to retrieve the information as needed. Although not required, the most effective way to manage your data is to structure it in a columnar format. This means the column headers on the first row of your spreadsheet would contain the titles of the data you plan to store and the subsequent rows below the column headers would contain the corresponding data.

Capturing information in this format not only makes it much easier to view your data on the spreadsheet but also makes working with arrays within your code, much easier.

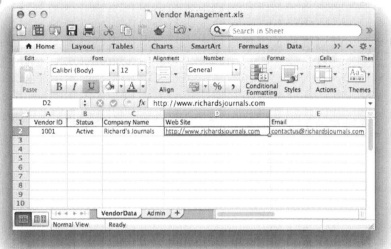

The User Form Image

By default, the User Forms you can create in the Microsoft Excel Visual Basic Editor environment is gray in color and very plain. The mostly square looking objects added to a User Form also leave a lot to be desired. The secret to creating a professional and more esthetically appealing User Form requires the use of an image.

The User Forms within this book consist of multiple images layered onto a background image. Based on the needs of your project you can choose to create individual buttons, labels, and images separately. Then piece them together during the User Form development process within Excel. The choice is a matter of preference.

You can choose any graphic editing software packages when creating an image. In this book, I chose to utilize the Adobe software suite that offers Fireworks and Photoshop. The individual software within the suite has their own unique set

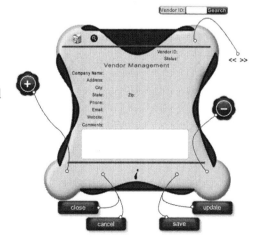

of tools designed to help anyone develop great looking images as seen below.

The following image consists of one large image and six separate images. Creating individual images will afford you the opportunity, through the use of code, to hide and display buttons based on the interaction with the User Form.

Various uses of a User Form

A User Form allows you to organize your data in an easy to read format. It can also be designed to allow you to send emails, open up web pages, delete/add records, filter, sort, view pictures, export data, print records, search records, view other User Forms, open documents and much, much more.

A User Form can be designed to display an employee's information along with their image or permit an administrator to track internal changes within the organization or simply to maintain someone's DVD collection. The combinations of designs and uses of a User Form is endless and only limited by your imagination.

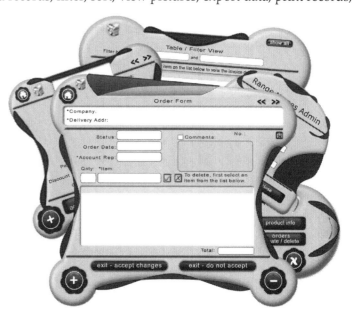

Save As

The .xls file format is compatible with Excel 97 through Excel 2003 for Windows and Excel 98 through Excel 2004 for Mac. Saving in this format will permit you to preserve the Visual Basic Application (VBA) macro code and Excel 4.0 macro sheets needed for creating User Forms. Therefore, when creating any User Form, make sure you save your Microsoft Excel workbook in the format .xls. Saving in this format will still permit you to create User Forms that can interact with newer versions of Office Suite Applications.

The Power of a Professional User Form

An interior designer utilizes color to psychologically help create the right mood for every room. The same can also be said about a well-crafted User Form. Carefully planning out and incorporating images, themes, color schemes, and font styles into your User Form will help you to create a unique aesthetically appealing User Form.

User Forms can come in different shapes, sizes and designs. The examples below demonstrate how you can use yellow fiberglass or stained wood grain to embellish your User Form appearance. Based on the same User Form layout, look closely at how each design expresses a different feeling.

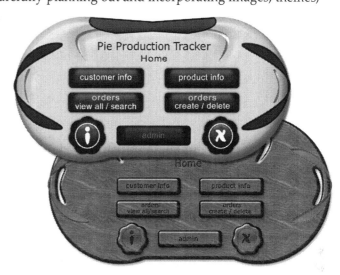

Parts of a User Form

Working with an Excel workbook can be somewhat overwhelming for people to navigate through. And if left unguarded the possibility for human error with the management of the data in your spreadsheets can be scary.   Utilizing a User Form is a great way to control the flow of information into and out of your Excel

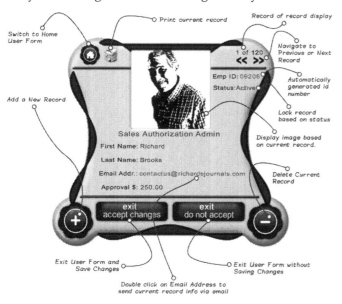

workbook. Through the use of an object on your User Form you can allow the user to go to the next record; previous record; print the current record; insert an image; save changes; delete a record or add a record. You can also create an object to search for an existing record within your data source or allow the user to navigate from one User Form to another.

Actions such as opening another application, auto-calculating, displaying lists, and incorporating your data as a data source to be used in e-mails or templates are just some of the many other options available within a User Form.

Chapter 2:
The Process

Where to begin?

Planning for success is the key element in the development of a User Form. It always serves a project well to begin the process by getting your thoughts out on paper. You want to identify the purpose of the User Form, the fields, the object and other bells and whistles to make available to the user of the User Form. With this information you are in a position to create a rough draft sketch of your User Form. Each step in the process is a valuable tool needed to help identify any possible flaws with the User Form prior to any development. Once you feel comfortable with the information gathered, you are in a better position to move forward with the development of the User Form.

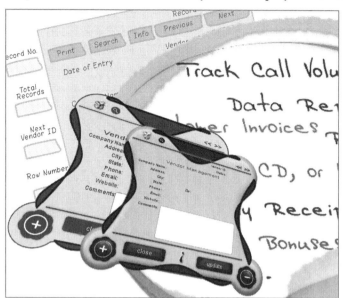

The details of the project development process are discussed further in detail in the next chapter.

Identify the Purpose of the Form?

Before you begin any project, always invest the time into gathering your thoughts. It is imperative that there is a clear focus and a goal in mind. So, with a pencil and paper in hand identify and apply the following planning process to your projects.

Understanding and identifying the purpose of the workbook and form is the first step of every project. Ask yourself, "Will the workbook or User Form be used for tracking customer calls, customer invoices, employee bonuses and so forth?" Try to be specific. By knowing this information it will help to set up the course of the planning process for your project.

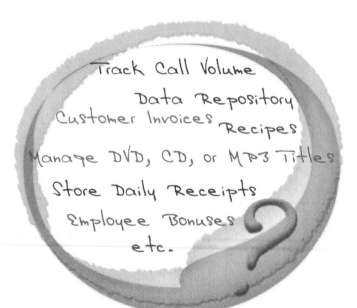

Brainstorm

After you have identified the purpose, it is necessary to brainstorm. You must think of every field and button you or the end-user would like to see on the workbook or User Form. Think of this as a wish list and write your thoughts down on paper, no matter how small and insignificant they may appear at first. Because you are brainstorming, you are writing down field names and types of buttons as they come to you and therefore in this phase, they are in no specific order.

FIELDS	BUTTONS	HIDDEN FIELDS
Vendor ID	Print	Record Number
Last Modified By	Previous Record	Total Records
Date Modified	Next Record	Next Vendor ID No.
Time Modified	Close	Row Number
Date of Entry	Cancel	Find Vendor ID
Status	Update	Set Focus
Company Name	Save	
Address	Delete Record	
City	Open/Close Search	
State	Search	
Zip		
Phone		
Email		
Website		
Comments		
Records Display		

If you are considering creating a workbook to track your company's vendors, then you might consider some of the field names referenced below. This process is the opportunity to think freely without any major concern for order.

When you become familiar with designing forms you will notice what is consistent between the different User Forms you create. Because most forms store records, certain types of buttons are required on the form to allow the end-user to navigate between the records; save changes; delete records; add records and print records. The hidden fields on the list below are objects designed to capture information so it can usually be manipulated with code for other purposes, or solely to be hidden from the user.

Identify Output Needs:
Filters, Queries, Graphs and Reports

Identify the types of filters, queries, graphs and reports you anticipate you want to retrieve from this workbook or User Form. In this phase your goal is to think of fields you might have overlooked during the brainstorming phase. If you expect to filter by the "State" field from your list then you must first make sure this field exists.

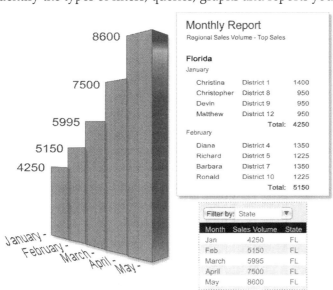

If you discover you are missing a field, you need to go back to the beginning. Starting the cycle all over helps you to rethink the direction you're going with this project. Trust me, it is well worth the effort to iron out these details at the very beginning. Continue through this process until you feel very comfortable that you have thought of every field before you move onto the Organize phase.

Organize Your Thoughts

Since brainstorming is considered unorganized and random thoughts, the next phase is to organize and streamline your list. For instance, if you listed "address" as a field you would like to create, ask yourself what "address" field means to you. Do you expect the user of your User Form to enter the entire address on one line or would you prefer to have separate lines for city, state, and zip. You want to be very specific.

The advantage to taking this approach is it makes it easier to either perform searches, refer to the individual fields in a report, or a filter. If necessary in the future, through the use of code, you may also combine the fields together into one field. The choice is purely a matter of preference.

Brainstorm	Organize Your Thoughts
Vendor ID	Vendor ID
Last Modified By	Last Modified By
Date Modified	Date Modified
Time Modified	Time Modified
Date of Entry	Date of Entry
Find Vendor ID	Find Vendor ID
Status	Status
Company Name	Company Name
Address	Address
	City
	State
	Zip
Phone	Phone
Email	Email
Website	Website
Comments	Comments
Records Display	Records Display

Rough Draft Sketch

A rough draft sketch of your User Form includes the fields you identified during the previous phases and gives you a visual perspective of your User Form layout. When sketching your User Form layout, always consider the field order when placing them on your User Form. For instance, place the fields on to the User Form in the order you would expect the user to enter the information.

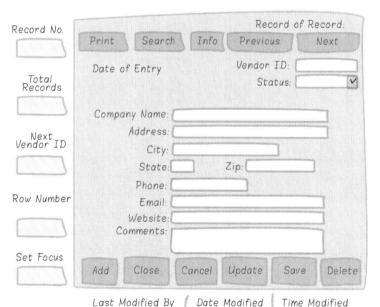

The rough draft is a great visualization tool. If you are a visual person such as I am, taking this approach will help you immensely. When you see it laid out, you can look at the overall project from many different points of view. In many cases, when all the fields that have been identified during the previous phases are laid out, you may notice you forgot to identify a field or you may determine there is no longer need for a field.

Include on your sketch any buttons, drop down lists, scroll bars and other items you are considering for your User Form. Focus only on the layout and do not worry about any coding that will be required for your User Form to work. We will address the coding aspect of your User Form in a later section.

User Form Image Layout

The functionality of a User Form will work the same if the User Form is generic looking with a simple square layout or enhanced with an image. Our goal is to enrich the end-users experience with their User Form by

providing an aesthetically pleasing User Form layout. One of the great advantages to working with an image is you can get very creative with your User Forms. Based on your rough draft sketch, you may begin to sketch a new layout with a more artistic design.

The Excel Visual Basic Editor allows you to use any combination of GIF, JPG and BMP images on your User Forms. Be aware, depending on the images you choose, the

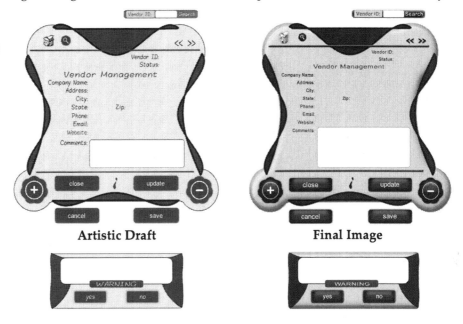

Artistic Draft   **Final Image**

Excel workbook, file size can increase or decrease. If file size is a concern, I encourage you to experiment with different image file types to determine which one works best for you and your project.

Using any software of your choice you can now create your image. The images for the User Forms referenced in this book have been created using Adobe Fireworks CS and Photoshop CS.

Identify Object types

This is the final phase of your planning before you begin developing your project. During this phase you are

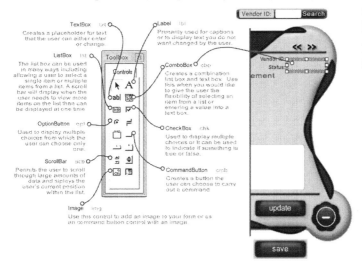

ready to identify the object types for your User Form. Decide which objects would best meet your needs based on the fields you identified for your User Form.

User Form Field Objects, Types and Names

When you identify the object type, it is time to also consider the name of the objects. A common practice is to add an abbreviated reference to the type of object at the beginning of the name. For example, a Text Box

UserForm Field Name	Object Type	Object Name
Vendor ID	TextBox	txtVendorID
Date Of Entry	TextBox	txtDateEntered
Find Vendor ID	TextBox	txtFindVendorID
Status	ComboBox	cboStatus
Company Name	TextBox	txtCoName
Address	TextBox	txtCoAddress
City	TextBox	txtCoCity
State	TextBox	txtCoState
Zip	TextBox	txtCoZip
Phone	TextBox	txtCoPhone
Email	TextBox	txtCoEmail
Website	TextBox	txtCoWebsite
Comments	TextBox	txtComments
Records Display	Label	lblRecOfRec
Record Number	TextBox	txtRecordNo
Next Vendor ID No.	TextBox	txtNextVendorID
Row Number	TextBox	txtRowNo
Set Focus	TextBox	txtFocusHere
Total Records	TextBox	txtTotalRecords

object storing phone numbers could be named txtPhone. When considering a name for your object, keep in mind you cannot use special characters; avoid spaces in the name; keep it short, simple and it should identify the data you plan to retrieve or store in the objects.

There is no right or wrong way when abbreviating the names for your objects. Just make sure the name makes sense to you or anyone else at first glance. You can keep all references to the objects type at the beginning of the object name in lowercase and the remaining abbreviated words can begin with a capital letter. This method can help you to differentiate between the object type and the object name.

Later in the book you will learn how to add code to your User Forms. Throughout your code you will notice the object names will be frequently referenced. So, therefore consider the name of the object very carefully and make all efforts to avoid changing it once you have decided on a name.

User Form Button Types and Names

You will soon discover the Image object can serve multiple purposes. Through the use of code you will learn

Object Action	Back Style	Object Name
Add Record	Image	imgAddRecordBtn
Background	Image	imgBackground
Cancel	Image	imgCancelBtn
Close	Image	imgCloseBtn
Delete Record	Image	imgDeleteRecordBtn
Info	Transparent	imgInfoBtn
Next Record	Image	imgNextRecordBtn
Open Search Toolbar	Transparent	imgOpenToolbarBtn
Previous Record	Image	ImgPrevRecordBtn
Print Current Record	Transparent	imgPrintRecordBtn
Save	Image	imgSaveBtn
Search	Transparent	imgSearchBtn
Search Toolbar	Image	imgSearchToolbar
Update	Image	imgUpdateBtn

to use transparent and regular images as buttons in place of the command button object. This is accomplished by overlapping the various images on top of the background image. The decision to use either option will be based on whether there is a need to disable, hide or display an image. Each approach is very effective.

NOTE
The BackStyle for an Image object is either transparent or opaque. The Image object will be clear when transparent or it will display an image when it is set to opaque.

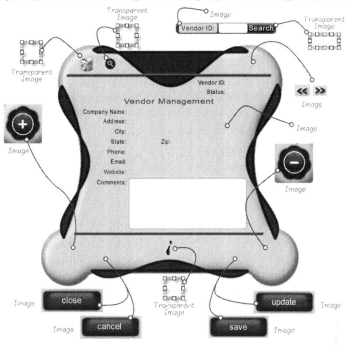

Identify Worksheet Formats and Column Header Names

Prior to creating your User Form, you have to prepare the workbook that will store the data you will capture with the User Form. During this phase it is important for you to start considering the column headers and cell formats for the Excel workbook.

FIELDS			
Worksheet	Cells	Field Name	Data Type
VendorData	A1	Vendor ID	Number
VendorData	B1	Last Modified By	Text
VendorData	C1	Date Modified	Date
VendorData	D1	Time Modified	Time
VendorData	E1	Date of Entry	Date
VendorData	F1	Status	Text
VendorData	G1	Company Name	Text
VendorData	H1	Address	Text
VendorData	I1	City	Text
VendorData	J1	State	Text
VendorData	K1	Zip	Text
VendorData	L1	Phone	Text
VendorData	M1	Email	Text
VendorData	N1	Website	Text
VendorData	O1	Comments	Text
Admin	A1	Status Options	Text
Admin	C1	Last Used Vendor ID	Number

Because the user normally has access only to the User Form the effort you place into formatting the workbook contents is primarily for your benefit. Formatting the cells make it not only visually appealing, but also ensure references made to the data in your workbook, such as through a report, is displayed correctly without much need to alter the appearance of the data.

The data type format you decide to use for each field will be applicable to the entire column storing the corresponding data. For example, to store phone numbers without a hyphen or parenthesis you set the column data type to number.

To view the available data types, open Excel and then select Format and Cells from the menu or press [Ctrl] and [1] simultaneously.

Getting a Second Opinion

Whenever possible, it is important to get a fresh perspective: a second opinion. Because you are very close to the project, your mind can sometimes become very narrow in its focus. A fresh set of eyes gives you a new viewpoint to ideas you had not yet considered. Plus, just because something on your list seems clear to you, it may not necessarily be clear to someone else. You need to know this valuable piece of information during the planning stage and correct it prior to creating your project. It is better to know at the beginning that something is not working properly rather than later.

Fields (UserForm / Worksheet)
- ✓ Vendor ID
- ✓ Last Modify By
- ✓ Date Modified
- ✓ Time Modified
- ✓ Date of Entry
- ✓ Status
- ✓ Company Name
- ✓ Address
- ✓ City
- ✓ State
- ✓ Zip
- ✓ Phone
- ✓ Email
- ✓ Website
- ✓ Comments
- ✓ * Status Options
- ✓ * Last Used Vendor ID

Image used as buttons
Transparent Images
- ✓ Print
- ✓ Open/Close Search Toolbar
- ✓ Info
- ✓ Search

Opaque (Regular) Images
- ✓ Previous
- ✓ Next
- ✓ Add Record
- ✓ Close
- ✓ Cancel
- ✓ Update
- ✓ Save
- ✓ Delete Record

**UserForm Hidden Fields
- ✓ Record Number
- ✓ Total Records
- ✓ Next Vendor ID Number
- ✓ Row Number
- ✓ Find Vendor ID
- ✓ Set Focus

* Located on the Admin tab in the Workbook and also referenced within the code.
** These fields will be hidden on the UserForm and the captured data will be referenced within the code.

If the project you are working on is for work then getting a second opinion and sign off on the project at this point is vital to the success of your project. Most importantly, a second opinion and sign off may avoid any unforeseen change of direction in the middle of development.

If the creation of your User Form is purely for personal reasons then consider this point in the process as a final checklist. Take on a dual role and give yourself some constructive criticism. Try to identify weaknesses in your list or User Form design. It helps to determine if there is a possible flaw in your project. To save you from a headache down the road, identify any issues and correct them before moving on to the development process.

Creating a Folder Structure

Only great things can come from being organized at the beginning of any project. Creating a solid folder structure makes it easy to find snippets of code, images, User Forms and other objects associated with your project.

Having a folder structure is not required when working with a project, nor is there a specific folder structure you should use. Referenced here is a suggestion for managing the items associated with the projects referenced in this book. You should consider making slight modifications to correspond with your projects as needed.

Folders
- Vendor Project
  - Code Snippets
  - Documents
  - Forms
  - Images
  - Modules

The folder structure you create in this book will be utilized during the development and testing phase of your project. When you are ready to use your completed User Form in production you want to create a new folder

structure to house only the User Form and workbook. Only you will need access to the images, documents and code snippets folder. To prevent unauthorized access or modifications, it should not be accessible in a public environment.

Vendor Project Maintain the Excel workbook and the following referenced folders.

Code Snippets Store all used and discarded pieces of code in this folder. Discarded pieces of code should be properly identified in the file along with embedded comments in the code specifying why the code is no longer part of your User Form. This approach will help you recall your thought process as to why the code did not work for your project and prevent you from repeating the same mistakes.

Documents Include any documentation related to the project within this folder. A good use for this folder is the storage of your project overview checklist and project specification documentation plus all of your development notes related to your project.

Forms Maintain all of the User Forms for your project here. This includes new and older User Forms. Prior to deleting any User Form from your project, you should save a backup copy of the User Form here.

Images Keep your original images such as PSD and PNG files here along with the final images used on your User Forms such as JPGs, GIFs and BMPs.

Modules Back up all modules referenced in your project.

Creating a Project Overview Checklist

The Project Checklist is a great asset in the development of any project. Maintaining a checklist at the onset of any project is an extremely valuable tool. The list helps you to identify all of the key variables of your project and it serves as a reference point during the coding and documentation phase.

Imagine the number of objects, names and pieces of code associated with a User Form or any given project. It only makes sense that sooner or later, if not properly tracked, you are going to confuse one name of an object for another and suddenly your code is not working. This type of error can become a nightmare to track down if you do not have a checklist to refer to. Future maintenance to your project can be greatly hindered because, without a checklist, you have to reacquaint yourself with the intricacies of a project and, if to much time has passed, you can easily forget why you decided to take the approach you did with your project. It is a must have for any project regardless of the size of your project.

Chapter 3:
Images

Creating User Form Images

Images available for download

The completed background image and the referenced buttons in this chapter are available for download at http://www.RichardsJournals.com.

On our website, locate and then select the Download option on our navigation bar. On the Download page, click on the book title "The Excel VBA User Form Conundrum Solved". **Prior to downloading and using the images please review and abide by the Terms of Use, the Permissions and Trademark guidelines on our site. The option to download the images will appear after you select the "Agree" button.**

Rough Draft

Imaged enhanced User Forms possess that "Wow" factor. Viewing a User Form with a great design always invokes a positive response from the user. As demonstrated below, a well-designed image can add a professional look and feel to your User Form. To begin the process of creating a User Form that looks great will require you to sketch your ideas into a rough draft format. This should take place during the planning stage of your project. Having this visual aid helps when it comes time to create your images regardless of what software you use.

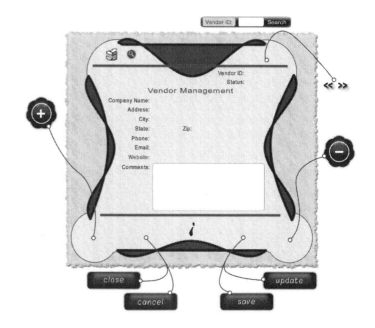

Based on the project specifications you may determine how many individual images need to be created for your User Form. For this project it has been determined there is a need for 10 individual images. There is the primary background image, search toolbar, previous record, next record, add record button, delete record button, close, cancel, update and save buttons.

Creating Images

The User Form images in this book have been created using Adobe Fireworks CS and Photoshop CS. Each application offers some great tools to help you create glass, wood, steel, plastic or any other combination of User Form styles. *Another alternative application you can consider, with far fewer tools and options, is the free GIMP*

GNU Image Manipulation Program. Familiarizing yourself with your choice of software will help you to create wonderful layouts for your User Form.

The Punch, Union and the Style tools in the Adobe Fireworks application was used to create the yellow plastic background image, buttons, and various other images referenced throughout this book.

Naming Convention

Consider utilizing a naming convention for your images. For example the images that will be used as buttons on the User Form will begin or end with Btn such as SaveBtn.jpg or BtnSave.jpg.

How to Create a User Form Background Image

You may use different variations of the built in punch, and union features along with unique styles to create some impressive User Form images. Based on your rough sketches and the purpose of the User Form you can determine if there is a need to create a single image or multiple images. The advantage to creating separate images is you can overlap them to create the illusion it is one image and then, through the use of code, you can hide each individual image based on code and specific user interaction with the User Form.

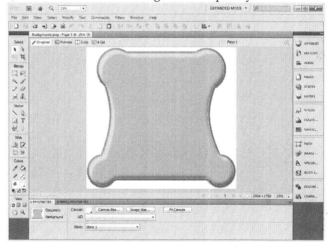

In this example, the punch and union technique is used to create the form below. The yellow plastic style was then applied to the image. Several images are then been combined to create the background image.

Techniques for Creating a Yellow Plastic Image

As referenced above with each step progression you will create the basis for the yellow plastic image.

Step 1   Set canvas size and then create a distorted square with rounded corners.

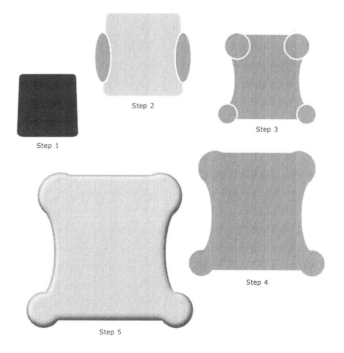

Step 1

Step 2

Step 3

Step 4

Step 5

Step 2   Overlap and individually punch out oval shapes from the newly formed square.

Step 3   Overlap circles and combine them individually by using the union feature.

Step 4   At this point you can optionally choose to save the completed image as a template to afford you the opportunity to apply various color combinations or themes.

Step 5   Apply styles to achieve the yellow plastic effect.

Setting the Canvas Size

The canvas is the area that will house the images you create within the Fireworks or Photoshop applications.

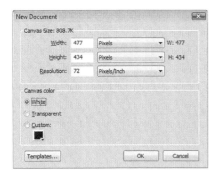

How to set the canvas size

1. Open Adobe Fireworks.
2. Select, Create New Fireworks Document (PNG).
3. The Canvas Size window will appear. Enter the following:
   3.1. **Width**: 477 Pixels
   3.2. **Height** 434 Pixels
   3.3. **Resolution** 72 Pixels/Inch
   3.4. **Canvas** color: White
4. Click on the OK button.
5. Save.

Punch

Using the punch feature allows you to remove portions of an objects path.

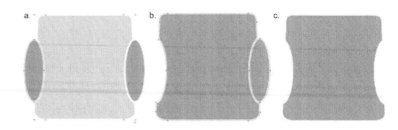

The goal is to take a top layer and punch out the design onto the bottom layer. To accomplish this in Adobe Fireworks you would select both the top layer and bottom layer, and then choose Modify, Combine Paths, and Punch from the menu bar.

NOTE   When using the punch feature you want to keep in mind the objects on the top layer will punch through items on the bottom layer. Select only one top layer and bottom layer at a time.

How to use the Punch feature

6. Select the Rounded Rectangle from the Tools toolbar and create a 368 pixels wide by 365 pixels high rectangle.

7. Center the rectangle on your canvas.

8. Add a new layer.

9. Select the Ellipse tool from the Tools toolbar and create two oblong circles 96 pixels wide by 233 high.

10. Position one oblong circle on each side of the rectangle.

11. Simultaneously select the rectangle, plus the Shift key and the oblong circle on the left side. Release the Shift Key.

12. With the items already selected, select Modify, Combine Paths and then Punch from the menu bar.

13. Repeat steps 5 and 6 for the oblong circle on the right side.

Union

Combine selected objects paths. To begin the process, select the individual objects and then select Modify, combine Paths and Union from the menu bar.

How to use the Union feature

14. Add a new layer.

15. Select the Ellipse tool from the Tools toolbar and create two circles 117 pixels wide by 117 pixels high.

16. Position one circle on the upper left side of the rectangle and the other on the upper right side.

17. Add a new layer.

18. Select the Ellipse tool from the Tools toolbar and create two circles 94 pixels wide by 94 pixels high.

19. Position one circle on the lower left side of the rectangle and the other on the lower right side.

20. Simultaneously select the rectangle, plus the Shift key and all of the circles.

21. With the items already selected, select Modify, Combine Paths and then Union from the menu bar.

Style

A style is a set of predefined strokes, filters, fill, and text attributes.

How to set the image style

22. Select the newly created image.

23. On the properties toolbar, select the Filters option.

24. Set the following filters for each referenced properties.

Inner Shadow

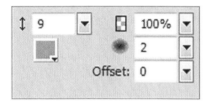

Inner Glow

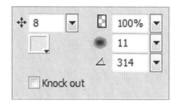

Inner Shadow

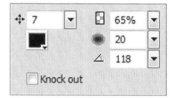

Hue/Saturation

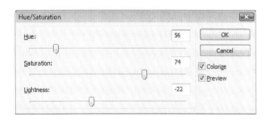

Brightness/Contrast

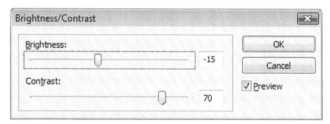

Curves

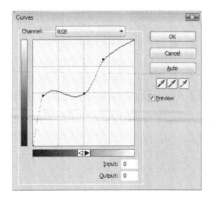

NOTE   Once you have created a style for your image you can save it to the Adobe Fireworks
                style library. The saved style can now be applied to other images you create.

Image Formats

Prior to creating the image, also consider the image format that you plan to use with the User Form. The size
of the image can also have
an impact on the size of
your Excel workbook file
size. In Fireworks this
can be set under the
"Optimize" window. The
final appearance of your
image may vary,
depending on the format
you choose; therefore, view the differences between the formats closely before making a decision.

362.97 k   19.92 k   65.13k

Export Image

How to export an Image

25. Select File, and then Export from the menu bar.

26. The Export window will open. If it does not, select Window and then Optimize from the menu bar.

27. Choose the Export File Format JPEG from the drop down list.

28. In the Save In field browse to the Images folder you created for your project.

29. Enter the File Name, Background and verify the Export field is set to Images Only.

30. Click the Save button.

Finishing Touches

The background image is the foundation of your User Form image. Layer the finishing touches such as trim lines, text labels, printer icons, info, search and other needed images onto your background image, to create one image.

As mentioned previously, the buttons for this User Form have been created separately. The images for each button are to be added individually during the designing phase of the User Form in the Excel VBE window.

Additional User Form Images

The User Form design below consists of ten individual images. There is a Vendor ID Search toolbar, background image, previous record button, next record button, add record button, delete record button, close button, cancel button, save button and an update button images. The separate images will be overlapped during the designing phase of your User Form and through the use of code they will be managed based on the actions of the user.

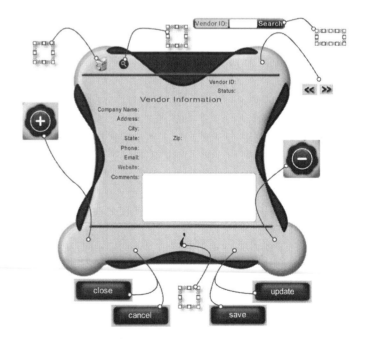

Create Button Images

NOTE   Excel does not offer the option to import an image with a transparent background. To work around this limitation the background of the buttons you create need to match the same color of the User Form background image. In this case it is a yellowish orange color.

Cancel, Close, Save and Update Button Images

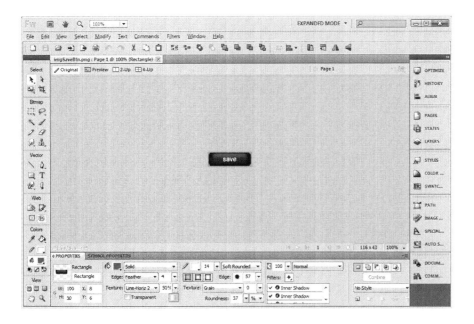

1. Open Adobe Fireworks.

2. Select, Create New Fireworks Document (PNG).

3. The Canvas Size window will appear. Enter the following:

    3.1. **Width**: 108 Pixels

    3.2. **Height** 38 Pixels

    3.3. **Resolution** 72 Pixels/Inch

    3.4. **Canvas** color: Custom #FEDF00 (The yellowish orange background is needed to match the background image color)

4. Click on the OK button.

5. Select the Rounded Rectangle from the Tools toolbar and create 100 pixels wide by 34 pixels high rectangle.

6. Center the rectangle on your canvas.

7. Select the newly created rectangle.

8. On the properties toolbar, select the Filters option and make the following changes for each of the following:

NOTE   Multiple Inner Shadow Filters are added to create a unique look for your image.

Inner Shadow
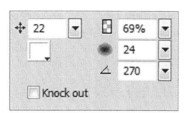

Inner Shadow
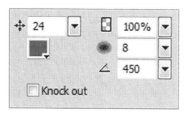

Inner Shadow
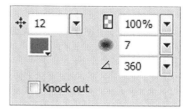

Inner Shadow
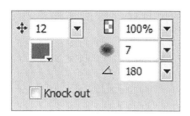

Inner Glow
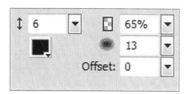

Hue/Saturation
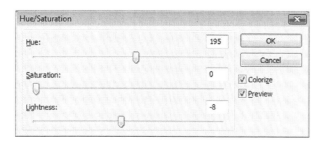

Curves
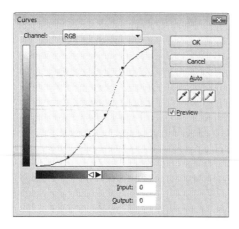

Add Text to Button Image

9. Add a new layer.

10. Select the Text Tool from the Tools toolbar and click on the center of the rectangle.

11. Type Save

12. Set the following for the text.

    12.1. **Font Family:** Arial

    12.2. **Font Style:** Regular

    12.3. **Font Size:** 15

    12.4. **Font Color:** White

    12.5. **Alignment:** Center

13. Type in Save for the text.

14. Repeat steps 7 through 10 for the Cancel, Update and Close button images and name them accordingly.

Export

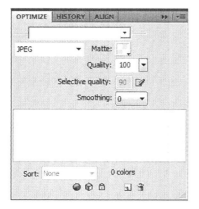

15. Select Window and then Optimize from the menu bar.

16. Choose the Export File Format JPEG from the drop down list.

17. Select File, and then Export from the menu bar.

18. The Export window will open.

19. In the Save In field browse to the Images folder you created for your project.

20. Enter the File Name as referenced on your checklist (example: SaveBtn) and verify the Export field is set to Images Only.

21. Click the Save button.

22. Repeat steps 2 through 21 for the Cancel (CancelBtn), Close (CloseFormBtn), Save (SaveBtn) and Update (UpdateBtn) button images.

Next Record and Previous Record Button Images

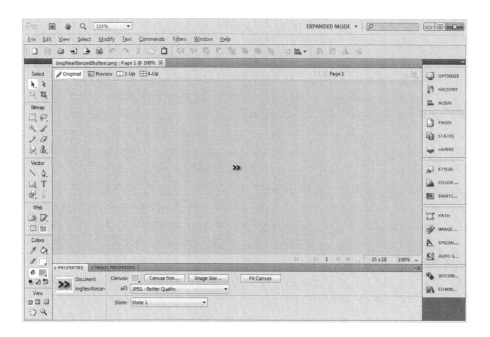

1. Verify Adobe Fireworks is open.

2. Select, Create New Fireworks Document (PNG).

3. The Canvas Size window will appear. Enter the following:

    3.1. **Width**: 25 Pixels

    3.2. **Height** 18 Pixels

    3.3. **Resolution** 72 Pixels/Inch

    3.4. **Canvas** color: Custom #FEDF00 (The yellowish orange background is needed to match the background image color)

4. Click on the OK button.

5. Add a new layer.

6. Select the Text Tool from the Tools toolbar and click on the center of the canvas. To create this image requires you enter the > character twice by pressing the Shift and the period "." keys simultaneously.

7. Center the text on your canvas.

8. Set the following for the text.

    8.1. **Font Family:** Bauhas 93

    8.2. **Font Style:** Regular

    8.3. **Font Size:** 18

    8.4. **Font Color:** Black

    8.5. **Alignment:** Center

9. On the properties toolbar, select the Filters option and make the following changes for each of the following:

Raised Embossed   **Drop Shadow**

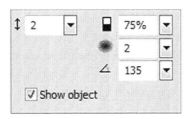   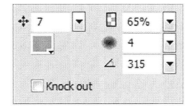

10. Select Window and then Optimize from the menu bar.

11. Choose the Export File Format JPEG from the drop down list.

Export

12. Select File, and then Export from the menu bar.

13. The Export window will open.

14. In the Save In field browse to the Images folder you created for your project.

15. Enter the File Name as referenced on your checklist (example: NextRecordBtn) and verify the Export field is set to Images Only.

16. Click the Save button.

17. Repeat steps 2 through 16 for the Previous Record button image (PrevRecordBtn), except, you will enter the < character twice, by pressing the Shift and comma "," key simultaneously.

Add and Delete Record Button Images

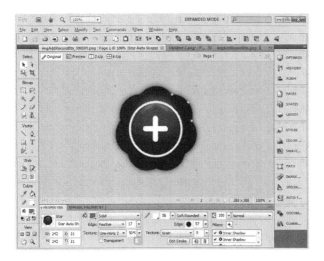

1. Verify Adobe Fireworks is open.

2. Select, Create New Fireworks Document (PNG).

3. The Canvas Size window will appear. Enter the following:

   3.1. **Width**: 69 Pixels

   3.2. **Height** 69 Pixels

   3.3. **Resolution** 72 Pixels/Inch

   3.4. **Canvas** color: Custom #FEDF00 (The yellowish orange background is needed to match the background image color)

4. Click on the OK button.

5. Add a new layer.

6. Select the Star Tool from the Tools toolbar and click on the upper left corner of the canvas and drag down to the lower right corner of the canvas. Drag the other associated points on the star to create a 7-rounded point star.

7. Verify the star is selected and then set the following properties.

Star Properties

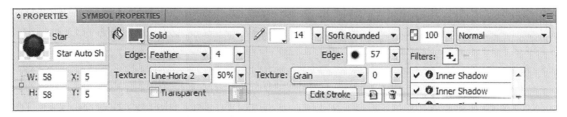

Inner Shadow

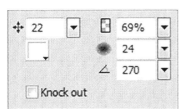

Inner Shadow

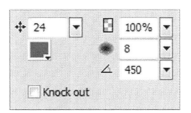

Inner Shadow

Inner Shadow

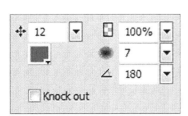

Inner Glow

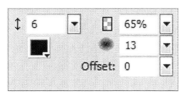

Hue/Saturation

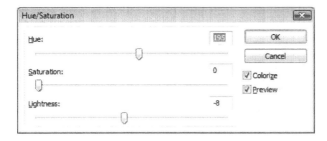

Curves

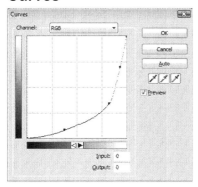

8. Add a new layer.

9. Select the Ellipse Tool from the Tools toolbar and click on the upper left corner of the canvas and drag down to the lower right corner of the canvas and create a white colored circle with a 37 width by 37 height dimensions.

10. Center the circle over the star.

11. Set the following properties for the circle.

Ellipse Properties

12. Add a new layer.

13. Select the Text Tool from the Tools toolbar and click on the center of the canvas. Add a plus symbol by selecting the Shift and equal "=" keys simultaneously.

14. Center the text between the newly added circle.

15. Set the following for the text.

   15.1. **Font Family:** Arial

   15.2. **Font Style:** Regular

   15.3. **Font Size:** 40

   15.4. **Font Color:** White

   15.5. **Alignment:** Center

16. Select Window and then Optimize from the menu bar.

17. Choose the Export File Format JPEG from the drop down list.

Export

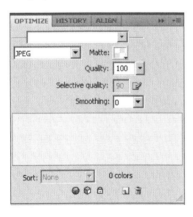

18. Select File, and then Export from the menu bar.

19. The Export window will open.

20. In the Save In field browse to the Images folder you created for your project.

21. Enter the File Name as referenced on your checklist (example: AddRecordBtn) and verify the Export field is set to Images Only.

22. Click the Save button.

23. Repeat steps 2 through 22 for the Delete Record (DeleteRecordBtn) button image, except, you will enter the minus symbol (aka hyphen character) which is located just to the left of the equal key.

Work Around

As mentioned previously, Excel does not offer the option to import an image with a transparent background. To work around this limitation and to ensure the separately created images blend perfectly with your background image you created for your User Form, consider the following shortcut.

This method can prove to be very effective for creating the illusion of images with a transparent background. For example images that contain shaded, curved, beveled or raised effects like the Add and Delete Record buttons referenced in this book.

1. Verify Adobe Fireworks Is open.

2. Open the background image you previously created.

3. Then create the Add and Delete button directly onto the background image by following steps 5 thru 15 as referenced under the Add and Delete Button Image section.

4. Then select all three images; add, delete and background images.

5. Group all of them together by selecting Modify and Group from the menu bar.

6. Now it is time to compress all images into one, also referred to as flattening the image. To do this, select Modify and Flatten Selection from the menu bar.

7. Select the newly flatten image and then select the Marquee Tool. Use the tool to trace out a 68 by 68 pixel size square over the Add Record button.

8. Cut out the image by selecting the [Ctrl] and [X] keys simultaneously.

9. Create a new document by pressing the [Ctrl] and [N] keys simultaneously. The canvas setting should default to the cut out image of 68 by 68 pixels. If it does, accept the default settings or adjust the size and then click Ok.

10. Paste the image and save it as AddRecordBtn.

11. Repeat steps 6 though 9 for the Delete Record button and save as DeleteRecordBtn.

Chapter 4:
The Basics

The Excel Workbook

There are certain basic key points you want to be familiar with when preparing a workbook for use with a User Form. Since the Excel workbook houses all of the information you enter into your User Form it can be considered and treated as a data repository. The code associated with your User Form eventually refers to the defined ranges, worksheet names, rows, columns and cells within the workbook;

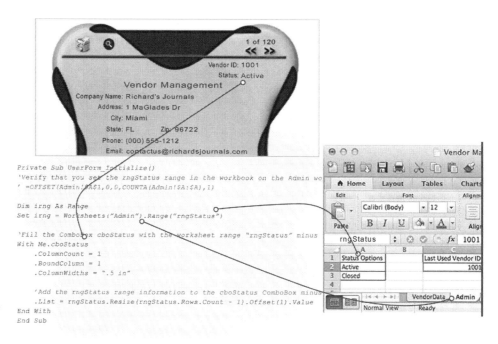

therefore the preparation of the work area within the workbook is considered a critical step in the overall development process.

In this example of a User Form with a Combo Box, the code references a named range and a worksheet name within the Excel workbook.

What is VBA?

Visual Basic for Applications is designed to permit you to manipulate objects in each Microsoft Office application. This is referred to as an "Object Model". Through the use of code, you may use individual properties and methods to capture events and actions that occur with individually selected objects.

Many objects within the "Object Model" also have child objects. For instance, a worksheet object is the child object of the application's parent object. The code reference for these objects can be listed as "Application.Worksheets".

Working with a Worksheet

Rename Sheet Tab Name

By default, Excel names each worksheet "Sheet" plus the order number in which you added the sheet to the workbook. You can expect to see "Sheet1", "Sheet2", and "Sheet3"in a new workbook. A newly added worksheet to the workbook would be titled "Sheet4", "Sheet5"and so forth.

The default title of a worksheet is non-descriptive and it is beneficial to you and your project to create a new name that identifies the data stored within the worksheet. One of the many places the worksheet name can be changed is in the workbook and in the Visual Basic Editor (VBE) Window. You can use Sheets("Admin").Select to reference a Sheet name in your code. However, this method only works provided the Sheet is not renamed. Therefore taking this approach with your code is not necessarily the best approach.

To manually change the worksheet tab's name, you can do any of the following:

- Double-click on the worksheet tab name. Type in the new name and then press [Enter].

- Right-click on the worksheet tab name and then select "Rename" from the shortcut menu. Type the new name and then press [Enter].

- Enter Sheet2.Name = "Admin" within your code.

Although you can use as many worksheets as you want with a User Form, for this project I chose to use only two worksheets and deleted the remaining one. The information on the worksheet will be laid out in a table type format. This means the field titles appear on the first row and the subsequent data is listed in the corresponding columns.

The code associated with this project references the workbook name, range names, worksheet names and cells.

Renaming a worksheet appears initially to be more of a cosmetic change but it truly has a far greater significance. The impact is much more important when it comes time to referencing it in your code. By default in the project explorer window within the VBE environment, a sheet name appears as Sheet1(Sheet1), Sheet2(Sheet2) and so forth.

In the VBE environment the Sheet objects consist of two parts. The name in the parenthesis is the worksheet name and the name outside the parenthesis is referred to as the sheets "Code Name". Renaming a worksheet in your workbook to "VendorData" appears as Sheet1(VendorData) in the project explorer window. In this example, the Code Name "Sheet1" remains the same if the worksheet is renamed, is moved or if other sheets are added in the workbook.

Sheets Index Number

We can also specify a sheet by using its Index number. A sheets Index number is determined by its position in the workbook. The first tab in the workbook is considered "Index number 1" and the next tab is "Index number 2" and so on. If you had a worksheet titled "Admin" and it was the first tab in your workbook, you could refer to it in code by using Sheets(1).Select. Once again this method, like the one mentioned before, is unpredictable, because the index number referenced could change when you add, move or remove a worksheet.

Sheets Code Name

Used as the preferred method, most seasoned developers reference the Sheet CodeName. The "Project Explorer" window in the "Visual Basic Editor" contains the unique CodeName of each worksheet in the workbook. The sheet CodeName is located to the left of the parentheses, and the sheet name is displayed within the parentheses.

By default, the CodeName mirrors the sheet name. For example, Sheet1 is displayed as Sheet1 (Sheet1). Unlike the Sheet Index Number, this unique CodeName does not change even if the sheet is moved, renamed or if other sheets are added. You can change the CodeName during the design phase by selecting the sheet in the "Project Explorer" and then modifying the (Name) field in the "Properties" window.

For example, to reference Sheet3 with the CodeName titled "Admin" you could use Admin.Application.ActiveCell = "Hello" in your code. This code enters the word "Hello" into the current active cell on Sheet3 with the CodeName Admin.

Hiding Worksheets

You will find hiding a worksheet is a great way to keep the end-users of your User Form from accidentally making modifications to important pieces of information within your workbook. You may also have a need to hide worksheets for cosmetic or confidential reasons. Identifying the purpose for hiding the worksheet helps you determine which method to use.

When referring to a hidden worksheet you can think of it in terms of temporarily hidden or very hidden. To say that a worksheet will simply be hidden implies you are okay with the idea of anyone who is using your User Form having the capability of utilizing the menu to unhide the hidden worksheets. Through the use of code a worksheet can be very hidden and it would not be accessible through the menu.

Regardless if a User Form is temporarily hidden or very hidden, the information in the hidden worksheet can still be referenced from other worksheets and workbooks.

Hiding a worksheet using the menu bar

1. Select the worksheet you want to hide.

2. Select Format, Sheet, and Hide from the menu bar.

Unhide a worksheet using the menu bar

1. Select Format, Sheet, and Unhide from the menu bar.

Using code to make a worksheet very hidden

- Sheet1.Visible = xlSheetVeryHidden

Using code to unhide a very hidden worksheet

- Sheet1.Visible = True

Use the Option Dialog window to hide worksheet tabs

The following method hides all the tabs in the workbook and displays only the active worksheet.

1. Select Tools, and Options from the menu bar.

2. Click the View tab in the Options Dialog window.

3. Uncheck the Sheet tabs box under the Window Options section.

VBA Code Note

There are a few ways to refer to a worksheet name in your code. You can reference the worksheet name, the code name or the index number. The index number is determined by its position in the workbook.

- Sheets("VendorData").Select
- Sheets(1).Select
- Sheet1.Select

Enter Column Headers

The information in the worksheets should always be stored in a table (columnar) format. The first row on your worksheet will consist of the titles identifying the corresponding data within that column. We refer to these titles as column headers. Since this type of database layout is for storing your raw data, there is no need to worry about the cosmetic look and feel of the data. Also, there is no need to bold information, color cells or add any other formatting to the data on the worksheet. The primary purpose for the worksheet is to act as a data repository for all the information you store and retrieve from your User Forms.

Enter Test Data

During the development of your User Form you will need to perform periodic testing. To assist you during your testing efforts you need to enter test data on your worksheet. The data you create should be specific to the information you plan to enter into that column. For instance, you would not enter a phone number into a name field. You would also not enter both the first and last name information into the last name field.

Although it makes no difference if you enter real or fictitious data, approach your method with caution. When developing you should try to stay away from what is known as "production data" or "real data". If you use real customer information and you begin to make changes to it, as is required with testing then you risk the chance you might forget to delete the modified information prior to publishing your User Form. As a result, if the User Form is then used with your test data in tact then you can run into serious problems trying to determine if the data in your User Form is the result of testing or is real data.

I choose to use fictitious data such as crazy names like Lounge Lizard, Widget ABC Corp. and phone numbers like (000) 555-1212. This way there is no mistake what is test data when taking this type of approach. It is important that you stick with the formatting you plan for your workbook. If you plan for the customer to enter the phone number as (000) 555-1212 and then store that information without the parenthesis and hyphen then make sure your test data is listed as 0005551212.

Working with Ranges

Range names help to simplify references to a range of cells, a constant, a formula or the content of a cell. A well-designed User Form utilizes a dynamic named range because it automatically expands or contracts based on the number of items in the referenced cells. These types of range names are not listed in the Name Box; however, typing the dynamic range name into the Name Box and pressing [Enter] highlights the defined range. To achieve this we utilize the OFFSET and COUNTA Functions in our Defined Named Range.

Range Name Rules

4. They are not case sensitive.

5. They must be unique names. It cannot resemble a cell name, cell address or reserved word.

6. Must either begin with a letter, an underscore (_) or a backslash(\).

7. Can contain 1 to 255 characters in length.

8. Single name letters are permitted except "R" or "C".

9. Range names can contain only the following characters.

    9.1   Letter characters between A to Z.

    9.2   Number characters between 0 to 9.

    9.3   Special characters . _ and ? are permitted.

10. Range names cannot contain any of the following.

    10.1   Spaces.

    10.2   Any mathematical symbols such as - +*/<> and %.

    10.3   The Special characters #, $, or &.

Dynamic Named Ranges

A dynamic named range automatically expands or contracts based on the number of items. These types of range names are not listed in the Name Box; however, typing the dynamic range name into the Name Box and pressing [Enter] highlights the defined range. The OFFSET() function is used in most dynamic ranges.

Setting the following formula to the defined rngStatus range makes it a dynamic range and therefore ensures that any items added in Column A are included in the rngStatus range.

=OFFSET(Admin!$A$1,0,0,COUNTA(Admin!$A:$A),1)

IMPORTANT NOTES

1. Because range names cannot contain spaces, you should consider using an underscore character in its place.

2. When referencing a tab name consisting of two or more words and spaces between the words, you need to use an apostrophe at the beginning and ending of the tab name in the OFFSET formula. If it is a single word, there is no need for an apostrophe.

3. This dynamic named range requires information in the first column for each record or else it won't display all records. It will stop at the last populated cell in the first column. As a result your list will display only the records for each row above the cell. Therefore reserve this column for a field you will need occupied for each record, such as an "Entered By", or "Date Entered" field.

How to Define a Range Name

In this example we are defining a range name for the Vendor Information that is managed on the "Vendor Data" tab.

11. Highlight the cells containing the Vendor data including the column headers.

12. Select Insert, Name, and Define from the menu bar.

13. Type "rngVendorInfo" in the "Names in workbook:" field.

14. Enter =OFFSET('VendorData'!$A$1,0,0,COUNTA('VendorData'!$A:$A),1) in the "Refers to:" field.

15. Click on the Add button and then click the OK button.

Visual Basic Editor (VBE)

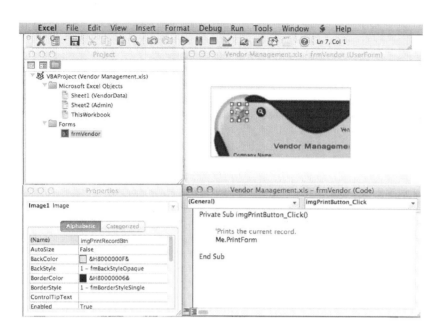

Very Important

File formats that work with Visual Basic

Excel 97 – 2004 Workbook.xls

This file format is compatible with Excel 97 through Excel 2003 for Windows and Excel 98 through Excel 2004 for Mac. Saving in this format will permit you to preserve the Visual Basic Application (VBA) macro code and Excel 4.0 macro sheets needed for the project referenced in this book.

Visual Basic Application Code (VBA) does not run in Excel 2008. Therefore, when creating the project in this book or your own, make sure you save your Microsoft Excel workbook as .xls format.

The Visual Basic Editor (VBE) is the environment used to manage, create, or modify macros in most Microsoft Office programs. A macro is a set of instructions referred to as code that is represented in an abbreviated format such as a subroutine. The code begins with the keyword "Sub" and ends with the keyword "End Sub". Modules consist of one or more macros, and projects can contain one or more modules.

A macro programming language used in Excel and other Microsoft Applications is referred to as Visual Basic for Applications also known as VBA. This type of code is contained within a macro. Different types of triggers such as command buttons, keyboard shortcuts and other VBA code can execute the macros.

The Visual Basic Editor can be accessed when Excel is open by selecting Tools, Macro, Visual Basic Editor from menu or by pressing [Alt] and [F11] keys simultaneously. The Visual Basic Editor is comprised of several different windows used to manage macros, properties, modules, projects and objects.

It is important to have a familiarity with the VBE environment. Within this area we work with the following: Project Explorer Window, the Properties Window, the Code Window and the Object Window. Although we will only focus on the windows and the objects pertaining to this project, you are encouraged to experiment and explore on your own as you become more familiar with the VBE environment.

How to open the Visual Basic Editor Window

1.   Verify Excel is open.

2.   To open the Visual Basic Editor you can perform either of the following:

   2.1   Select Tools on the menu bar, point to Macros, and then click Visual Basic Editor.

   2.2   Select View on the menu bar, point to Toolbars, and then click Visual Basic. When the toolbar appears point and click the Visual Basic Editor button.

   2.3   Press the [Alt] and [F11] keys simultaneously.

Explore the Visual Basic Editor Window

By default the Visual Basic Editor Window consists of three windowpanes. There is the Project Explorer Window, the Properties Window, and the Code Window. The Object Window is another window you will use and is only visible when you have selected a User Form in the Project Explorer Window. Each window is a docking panel that can be adjusted in size, dragged to another location within the Visual Basic Editor Window or detached as a floating panel for easier viewing.

The Project Explorer Window

This window displays by default when opening Visual Basic Editor and is primarily used to navigate throughout the different components of the project. The Project Explorer Window is laid out in a hierarchal

structure. All open workbooks and their associated worksheets are displayed in the Project Explorer Window along with Modules, Hidden Workbooks, Add-ins, and User Forms. Each open add-in and workbook in the Project Explorer Window is referred to as a project. You will use this window to navigate between the objects and code within your project.

Navigating the Project Explorer Window

1. There are three buttons at the top of the Project Explorer Window. Based on your selection in the Project Explorer Window you can view the following when you click on the corresponding buttons:

    1.1   Clicking the View Code button displays the Code Window for the selected object.

    1.2   Clicking the View Object button displays either the selected Object (Sheets) or User Form in the Object Window.

    1.3   Clicking the Toggle Folders button displays all objects, User Forms and modules in a list view.

    1.4   Clicking the Toggle Folders button again groups the items into objects, User Forms and Modules.

NOTE	Keep in mind regardless of how you rearrange your worksheets, when a sheet is created it maintains the original sheet name associated with it when you added the worksheet.

How to open the Project Explorer Window

1. Verify Excel is open.

2. Press the [Alt] and [F11] keys simultaneously to open the Visual Basic Editor.

3. By default the Project Explorer Window is located in the upper left corner windowpane. If the Project Explorer Window is not open then you can do any one of the following:

    3.1   Press the [Ctrl] and [R] keys simultaneously.

    3.2   Select View, Project Explorer on the menu in the VBE Window.

The Properties Window

This window displays the properties for any selected object. In the Properties Window you can modify the following: name, back color, border color, border style, font, fore color, height, width, positioning as well as many other attributes of a selected object. With some creativity you can make some great looking, user-friendly and functional User Forms.

If you have envisioned a certain look for your User Form, you will rely heavily on the Properties Window to achieve this look. An even slight, simple enhancement to objects helps to fine-tune a User Forms aesthetic look. Amongst all of the available attributes, I can modify in the Properties Window, I have found the positioning, height and width gives me greater flexibility over the objects on my User Form and allows me to get the exact specifications I need for my User Forms.

Navigating the Properties Window

1. The Properties Window displays all of the attributes of a selected object, User Form or object.

2. The Properties Window consists of two tabs.

    2.1   The Alphabetic tab lists the objects attributes in alphabetical order.

    2.2   The Categorized tab displays the objects attributes in group order by category. Each category group can be expanded or collapsed by selecting the button to the left of the category name.

NOTE   To avoid changes to the wrong object, it is imperative to verify your selection as identified in the (Name) field in the Properties Window prior to making changes to any attributes.

How to open the Properties Window

1. Verify Excel is open.

2. Press the [Alt] and [F11] keys simultaneously to open the Visual Basic Editor.

3. By default the Properties Window is located in the lower left corner windowpane. If the Properties Window is not open then you can do any one of the following.

    3.1   Press the [F4] key.

    3.2   Or you can select View and then Properties Window on the menu in the VBE.

The Code Window

Visual Basic Applications (VBA) code is maintained and modified within this window. As the name implies the Code Window displays all of the code associated with your project. The Code Window is accessible via a menu, toolbar, or shortcut keys. Along with entering code you can also enter comments in this window.

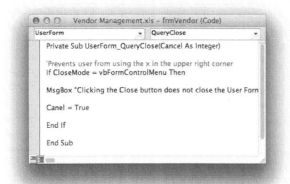

Working with the Code Window

1. You can do the following to view the code of any selected object.

1.1   Double click an Object or Module in the Project Explorer Window to view the associated code.

1.2   Right click an object, sheet or module in the Project Explorer Window and select View Code from the shortcut menu.

1.3   Click on the View Code button at the top of the Project Explorer Window after selecting an object, User Form or module in the Project Explorer Window.

1.4   Press the [F7] key to view the code of any selected object in the Project Explorer Window.

1.5   Select View, Code on the menu in the VBE Window after selecting any object in the Project Explorer Window.

1.6   Double click a User Form or the User Form Object(s) in the Object Window to access the corresponding code.

2. Any text following an apostrophe is converted to a comment.

3. Comments are considered informative text and it does not have an affect on the operation of the code.

4. By default comments entered in the Code Window are displayed in green font.

How to open the Code Window

1. Verify Excel is open.

2. Press the [Alt] and [F11] keys simultaneously to open the Visual Basic Editor.

3. By default, the Code Window is located on the right side of the Visual Basic Editor window.

The Object Window

The Object Window only displays when a User Form is selected in the Project Explorer Window. The creation of your User Form and objects occurs in this window. Think of the Object Window as the canvas for your project. The Object Window is only available when a User Form exists within your project.

Working with the Object Window

A User Form must exist within your project before you can utilize the Object Window.

1. You can do the following to view any User Form in the Object Window:

    1.1   Double click the User Form in the Project Explorer Window.

    1.2   Right click the User Form in the Project Explorer Window and select View Object from the Shortcut menu.

    1.3   Click the View Object button at the top of the Project Explorer Window after selecting the User Form in the Project Explorer Window.

    1.4   Select a User Form in the Project Explorer Window and then press the [Shift] and [F7] keys simultaneously to view the selected User Form in the Object Window.

How to open the Object Window

1. Verify Excel is open.

2. Press the [Alt] and [F11] keys simultaneously to open the Visual Basic Editor.

3. Select Insert and User Form on the menu in the Visual Basic Editor Window. The Object Window automatically opens with the newly added User Form in view.

4. By default the Object Window is located on the right side of the Visual Basic Editor window.

Deleting a User Form or Module

There is a time in many projects where you may need to delete an existing User Form or module. VBE recognizes you may have a change of heart or a need to refer to your deleted items at a later time. Therefore, any attempt to delete a User Form or module causes a message prompt window to display, at which time you can choose to export the item before removing it. I am very cautious by nature and I usually choose to export any item I am considering removing from my project before deleting it. I also add very detailed comments to any User Form or code I selected for deletion so I can refer to it a later time, if necessary. It helps to refresh my memory why a particular User Form or code did not work or no longer had a purpose any longer within my project. Refer to the section "Managing Folders" in this book for hints on a folder structure for any exported items within a project.

The Toolbox

This toolbar displays the Visual Basic standard object, including any ActiveX objects and any object you have added to your project. The toolbox toolbar is only visible when a User Form or object is selected. Right clicking the toolbox permits you to also add additional objects. Everything your User Form is to become is sculpted from the toolbox. I try to incorporate as many as I can in a project, where warranted, to bring strength and flexibility to my User Form designs. A well designed User Form with flexibility usually comes from converting an object intended for one purpose and using it for another. The prime example of this is converting an image into a button. The fun is exploring and delivering the unexpected.

Working with the Toolbox Toolbar

1. The Toolbox toolbar displays only when a User Form or the User Forms Objects is selected in the Objects Window.

2. If you have selected a User Form and the Toolbox toolbar is not visible, you can do the following:

    2.1   Select View and Toolbox from the menu in the VBE Window.

    2.2   Select the Toolbox icon on the Standard toolbar.

How to access the Toolbox Toolbar

1. Verify Excel is open.

2. Press the [Alt] and [F11] keys simultaneously to open the Visual Basic Editor.

3. Verify a User Form already exist within your project in the Project Explorer Window. If it does not exist, select Insert and User Form on the menu in the Visual Basic Editor Window.

4. To view the Toolbox toolbar double-click a User Form in the Project Explorer Window.

5. If the Toolbox toolbar does not display after double-clicking the User Form, then follow the directions above in the section Working with the Toolbox Toolbar.

Get Help

The VBE window is where you want to search for help when you need information specifically related to that environment. Do not underestimate the power of the Help feature in the VBE window. Keep in mind there are two very powerful search areas that exist within Excel, one is in the workbook view and the other is in the VBE environment. Both contain vastly different pieces of information. You would be surprised to discover in most cases the information you normally search on the web for, as it relates to a piece of code, how an object works, or an explanation of something in the VBE environment, is at your fingertips in the Help window.

How to access Help

1. Verify Excel is open.

2. Press the [Alt] and [F11] keys simultaneously to open the Visual Basic Editor.

3. Select Help and then Microsoft Visual Basic Help on the menu in the Visual Basic Editor Window or press F1.

Verify References Established

Before beginning any coding, you want to establish the references in the Visual Basic Environment. Overlooking this vital step can cause frustration when it comes time to run your code, which includes references to objects in other Microsoft applications. For instance, if your User Form includes an e-mail address and you would like to allow the user the capability to click the e-mail address and have Outlook automatically open, then this would require a reference to the Outlook library.

How to access the Reference Window

1. Verify Excel is open.

2. Press the [Alt] and [F11] keys simultaneously to open the Visual Basic Editor.

3. Select Tools and References on the menu in the Visual Basic Editor Window.

Chapter 5:
User Form & Objects

Inserting a User Form

Breaking Apart a User Form

Adding Objects

Working with an Image Object

How to Insert Text Box Objects

Working with Combo Box and Label Objects

Mouse Pointers (Cursors)

Managing Objects

How to Set Tab Order

Inserting a User Form

In conjunction with the code, the User Form is the basis of everything important to your project. Therefore, we want to develop a user-friendly interface that conforms to your needs or the needs of your customer. The

basic default tools provided in the Visual Basic Editor window is sufficient to create a generic User Form. A modification to the User Form properties permits you the opportunity to make enhancements that allow you to create aesthetically pleasing User Forms.

By default when you add a new User Form, a generic dialog box is created. Although the User Form would be completely functional as is, it is not aesthetically pleasing. Our goal is to create a user-friendly, eye-appealing, fully functional User Form. Remember, adding a well designed image greatly enhances the appearance of your User Form.

For the project in this book the image serves two purposes. The primary use is to display an image on your User Form. The second is to use an image in place of a command button. For instance, the Command button object on the Toolbox toolbar is also a generic object with cosmetic limitations. To work around this, you can incorporate transparent images with coding to create buttons for your User Form.

Breaking Apart a User Form

For the project referenced in this book you will create a Vendor Management User Form. This User Form consists of fourteen Image objects, one Combo Box object, one label object and sixteen Text Box objects. Through the use of code twelve of the Image objects will be converted to buttons.

The Toolbox Toolbar is used to create objects on a User Form. There is no specific order required when adding objects to a User Form. All objects have many attributes associated with them that can be modified.

Working with a User Form

All of the User Form background images referenced in this book contain the labels for all of the referenced text fields. This approach prevents the need to create individual labels for each Text Box object on the User Form; however, if you plan to hide your labels via code, you may want to create the labels at the time of design rather than making them part of your background image.

NOTES

- A User Form utilizing objects from other Microsoft applications require establishing the associated References in the Visual Basic Editor Window.

- You can have multiple User Forms in the same project.

- User Forms have minimize, maximize and close buttons. With code you can restrict the use of these buttons.

- Although a User Form property has the option to incorporate a picture directly into the background, I have chosen to utilize the Image object to create the background image. Taking this approach provides more flexibility.

- Through the use of code the Excel workbook can be hidden leaving only the User Form visible.

Adding Objects

The objects you add to your User Form are based on the fields you identified during your planning phase. To help you decide which object would best meet your needs, ask yourself the following questions:

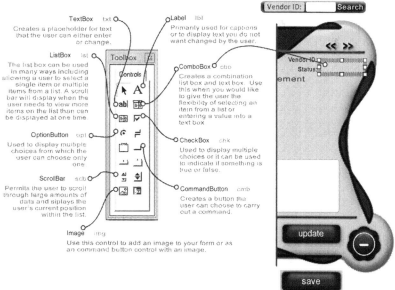

Possible Object Type Considerations

1. Will the user need to enter data into a field? For example will you enter a name? **Text Box**

2. Do you want to limit the user to a specific list? **Combo Box**

3. Does the user need to answer only yes or no as their response? **Check Box**

4. Do you need to provide instructions to the user or add a label? **Label**

5. Is an image needed? **Image**

6. Do you need the user to click a button to perform a specific action? **Command Button**

Working with an Image Object

Technically you could choose to import an image directly into the background of your User Form. This approach limits how you can control the image in the background. Instead you may choose to incorporate an Image object to hold the User Form image. With coding you would have the flexibility to hide the User Form, lock the User Form, and do many other things when necessary.

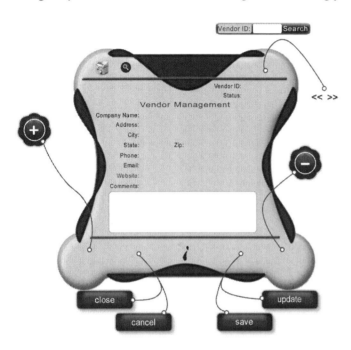

When creating a button, you can choose to use an Image object and select an image or you can make an Image object transparent and set it over an existing image. Your project and the action you are trying to achieve with your button will dictate what approach will work best for you. With coding either one is acceptable.

The acceptable images in a User Form are limited to Bitmap (BMP), JPEG (JPG), or GIF. The image size differs greatly between them. I stay away from Bitmaps because of their pixilation and size issues. I tend to utilize a combination of JPG's, or GIF images in the User Form I create.

The type of image you choose for your project should be weighed carefully when the size of your Excel workbook is an issue. The type of image you choose is just a matter of preference, but do keep in mind the Excel workbook file size can increase or decrease depending on what image file you are using: GIF, BMP or JPG image.

If file size is a concern, I would recommend experimenting with different image file types to see which one works best for you and your project.

I used Adobe Fireworks CS and Photoshop CS to create the images for the Excel VBA User Form referenced in this book.

NOTES

- In the Picture field of the Image object properties prior to selecting an image, the word by default (None) will appear in the field. After you select an image in the Picture properties field the word (Bitmap) appears in the field, regardless if you selected a JPG or GIF image.

- On occasion when you add an Image object to a User Form, the object is outlined but it seems to be hidden behind the User Form. If this occurs, verify the newly added object is selected and then choose Format, Order and Bring to Front (Press the [Ctrl] and [J] keys simultaneously) on the menu in the Visual Basic Editor Window. You could achieve the same results if you select the User Form and choose Format, Order and Send to Back (Press the [Ctrl] and [K] keys simultaneously) on the menu in the Visual Basic Editor Window.

- A shaded border with small boxes displays around the selected objects. Click and drag the border of the selected object to relocate it anywhere on the User Form.

- To manually adjust an object's, height and width point, left click and drag on any one of the small boxes on the border of an object. Adjustments to the Left, Top, Height and Width object properties are more accurate than manual adjustments to an object.

Transparent Background

By default when you open a User Form it will display within a square frame window. To hide the window and display only the User Form, you can utilize code to create a transparent background. To achieve this effect would require you to add the image directly to the User Form background instead of using the Image object. To do this you would select the User Form in the Object window and then click on Picture attribute in the properties window.

How to Add Remaining Objects to User Form

Now that you have the images and buttons added to our User Form it is time to add the remaining objects as needed for our project.

One Combo Box object and one Label object are needed for this project. Keep in mind had we not included the text labels on our User Form background image we would have needed to create additional Label objects to coincide with our Text Box and Combo Box objects.

To maintain an uncluttered area the hidden Text Box objects are positioned in the white spaces of the User Form background image to prevent objects from overlapping on the User Form.

Although some of the referenced Text Box objects are hidden, your project is best served if you keep a specific order of the tab index to prevent confusion. The TabIndex property specifies the tab order based on 0 to less than the number of objects on the User Form that has a TabIndex property. The tab index for the visible objects is okay from 0 to 9. It is good practice to list the hidden Text Box objects tab index at the end of the tab order; therefore, the remaining hidden objects tab index will be from 10 to 14 and the TabStop property will be listed as false.

How to Insert Text Box Objects

NOTE   If necessary you can increase or decrease the Left and Top Text Box object properties as needed to position the Text Box object to the right of the corresponding label.

1. Verify the User Form displays in the Object Window to the right of the Visual Basic Editor Window.
2. Click the User Form to verify it is selected.

3. Click the Text Box object once on the Toolbox Toolbar.

4. Then click once on the center of your User Form. This adds the object to your User Form.

5. Verify the newly added Text Box object is selected and then make the following changes to the Text Box properties in the Properties Window.

Working with Text Box Objects

An object placed onto a User Form assumes the User Form settings; therefore, when you change the User Form's font all newly added objects will use the new settings. To avoid the tedious process of modifying the font properties of each newly added Text Box object, it serves you best to make the change to the User Form font properties at the beginning prior to adding objects to your User Form. By default each newly added Text Box object will have the new font properties based on the User Form properties.

From time to time after you make a change to a Text Box object font or font size and after you enter text into the object you may notice that the font or font size did not change. Sometimes to correct the problem you need to first delete the Text Box object with the problem. Then add a new Text Box object, and try to make changes to the Font property again.

NOTES

- Do not be surprised if this approach does not correct the problem. When I first began to create User Forms, I became frustrated with the problems I experienced with modifying the Text Box objects, font and size properties. The changes would sometimes work and other times it would not work without any rhyme or reason. The best approach I found that works for me is to use code in the User Form Initialize section of the User Form. The Code section in this book displays this approach.

- Prior to making changes to individual object properties, determine if there are like changes for like objects. For instance, if you notice you plan to make every Text Box object with a transparent background and border style, then you would be better off making that change with code and placing it in the User Form Initialize area.

- By default when you add a Text Box object to a User Form each object will have a border with a white background. If you prefer less clutter on your User Form, then you might want to make each individual object transparent in the Design view instead of relying on code in the User Form Initialize section of your code.

A combination of the following Text Box object properties can greatly enhance the appearance or functionality of your object.

AutoSize	Automatically resizes the length of an object to display its entire contents. By default the box appears relatively small until text is added and then the object increases in size horizontally.
AutoTab	Automatically moves the cursor to the next object in the tab order when the maximum allowable number of characters are entered into the Text Box or Combo Box objects.

Enabled	Setting the value in this property to True permits the object to receive focus and respond to user entries. Setting the value to False prevents any direct interaction to this object on the User Form but is still accessible through code.
Font	Sets the font, font style, size and effects.
ForeColor	Sets the font color.
MaxLength	Sets the maximum number of characters in a field. You can enter a specific numeric to restrict how many characters a user can enter into a field.
MultiLine	This property works in conjunction with the WordWrap property. For this property to work the WordWrap field should also be set to True. When text is entered into a Text Box object that has a height greater than twice the size of the default height, then the text automatically wraps to the next line. If the ScrollBar property is set, then the scrollbars automatically display when the text entered into a Text Box is greater than the height of the Text Box object.
PasswordChar	The Character you enter in this property displays as a placeholder character instead of the characters actually entered in the Text Box. If you chose to enter the # character into this property then this character displays for each character you entered into the Text Box object. Any single numeric or text character can be entered into this field.
ScrollBar	You can set the Scrollbar in a Text Box object to none, horizontal, vertical or both.
TabIndex	Specifies the tab order based on 0 to less than the number of objects on the User Form that have a TabIndex property. No two objects can contain the same TabIndex number. For example, if you already have an object with a TabIndex of 5 and attempt to list the TabIndex for another object as 5 then the other object automatically changes to 6 and the remaining objects above the TabIndex of 6 moves up one number.
TabStop	Determines if an object receives focus when the user tabs to it.
Value	Sets the default value for the object. If you had a Text Box object to capture the Country of Origin and all of your customers are in the US then you could list US in the Value property to ensure the word US always displays in this object.
Visible	Determines if an object should be visible or hidden to the user.
WordWrap	This property works in conjunction with the MultiLine property. For instance if the MultiLine property is set to True and the WordWrap property is also set to True then any text entered into the Text Box object wraps the text to the next line.

Working with Combo Box and Label Objects

Most of the Text Box object properties are consistent with the Combo Box object properties. Referenced below are some of the Combo Box object properties that can be help you enhance the appearance of the drop-down list and specify other characteristics.

BoundColumn This property identifies which value to store a selected row in a multicolumn Combo Box. If you have a Combo Box with three columns listing the employee's first name in the first column, the employee's last name in the second column, and the department name in the third column and the BoundColumn is 2, and then based on the row you select, the employee's last name is the stored value.

ColumnHeads Displays the first row of data in your Combo Box object list as the column headings. The column headers cannot be selected.

ColumnWidths Entering a numeric value specifies the width of each column in a multicolumn Combo Box object. A semicolon separates the column width for each column (;). No value listed in the ColumnWidth field defaults to a width of 90 points (1.5 inches). To hide a column you must enter zero (0) as the value. To hide the second column in a three column Combo Box you would list the following ColumnWidths as 40;0;25.

DropButtonStyle Specifies the symbol of the drop-down button in a Combo Box. By default the DropButtonStyle value is 1-fmDropButtonStyleArrow by default. You can choose from an ellipsis (...), underscore character or no symbol.

ListRows A numeric value specifies the maximum number of rows displayed in a list. By default, 8 is value listed in the ListRows property. A vertical scroll bar displays when the number of items in the list exceeds the value of the ListRows property.

ListStyle You can change the cosmetic appearance from the default plain view to a list with option buttons located to left of each item in the list.

ListWidth A numeric value specifies the viewable width of the list in a Combo Box after the drop-down button has been selected. To view all of the columns in a multicolumn list, the value in this property should include the total values of all of the values referenced in the ColumnWidth property plus enough space to compensate for the space of the vertical scroll bar.

Locked Listing the property as True prevents the user from editing the value in the object.

RowSource Specifying a worksheet range provides a source for the Combo Box list. For example you could enter the following to display the values in range a2 to a4 on the frmInvoice worksheet. =frmInvoice!$A$2:$A$4 . If you decide to set the ColumnHeads property to True then the cell A1 on the frmInvoice worksheet in our example becomes the column header of your Combo Box list.

ShowDropButtonWhen Specify when the drop down button should be displayed. By default the property is set to 2-fmShowDropButtonWhenAlways. You can decide to never show the drop down button or only display the button when the object has focus.

Labels

You might be surprised to know the label object offers much more than you might think. The name, as it implies, is used as a label for objects. Labels along with coding can be used to create progress indicators, record x of y, and to display results from other objects.

Mouse Pointers (Cursors)

In simplest terms a cursor is a pointer that indicates a position on the screen. All of us are familiar with the white arrow that appears when we want to select an item from a menu or an object. By default Microsoft Windows provides us with a variety of cursor images that display based on what item our cursor is hovering over. With many programs, and on the web, many people have become accustomed to the idea of the pointer changing to a hand indicating it is an item you can click. In the VBE environment you have the option to choose the default Window cursors or you may create your own.

Here are the available cursors in the properties window in VBE.

0 - fmMousePointerDefault

1 - fmMousePointerArrow

2 - fmMousePointerCross

3 - fmMousePointerIBeam

6 - fmMousePointerSizeNESW

7 - fmMousePointerSizeNS

8 - fmMousePointerSizeNWSE

9 - fmMousePointerSizeWE

10 - fmMousePointerUpArrow

11 - fmMousePointerHourGlass

12 - fmMousePointerNoDrop

13 - fmMousePointerAppStarting

14 - fmMousePointerHelp

15 - fmMousePointerSizeAll

99 – fmMousePointerCustom

Managing Objects

When you have added objects to your User Form, you may have a need to resize or realign them. To accomplish this you may choose to do this manually or through the use of the Properties window. These changes can be made to a single object or to multiple objects at the same time. Lack of detail such as aligning your objects or ensuring all of the single line Text Boxes are the same size will be very noticeable and will severely impact visually an otherwise nice looking User Form.

How to Modify Object(s)

To align an object or a group of objects, you must first select the object. To select an object, you may click it or choose the name of the object from the Properties window. To select multiple objects, you may select the first object and then hold down the [Ctrl] key and click each additional object as needed. Another option to select multiple objects is to drag the objects you would like to select. To deselect any object, click any other object.

Position Objects

To align objects to each other, after you have selected two or more objects, you may right-click any of the selected objects, point to align on the shortcut menu and then choose the alignment of your preference. To align objects to the User Form, select the objects and then point to Center in the User Form on the menu bar and choose your alignment preference. With one or more objects selected you may also choose to drag the objects or modify the top or left format option on the Properties window for the selected objects. Although the Properties window provides precise alignment for the left and top axis you will not be able to use the undo feature, as you will with the other alignment options.

> **NOTE**   Some objects such as MultiPage, can only be repositioned from selecting the boxes around the border of the object and then dragging.

Adjust Size

Adding an object to a User Form is as easy as selecting an object from the toolbox and then clicking anywhere on the User Form. This produces a generic-sized object. Most of the time you may have to adjust the default size because the generic size is not sufficient for your needs. To achieve this, point to any one of the selected object border handles and drag it to the desired size. For a more consistent and precise layout of your objects you may adjust the width and height in the Properties window of the selected objects.

Another option for two or more selected objects is to select Format, Select same Size and the option of your choice from the menu bar. In some cases it is beneficial to accept the default height of a Text Box field and set the AutoSize property in the Properties Window to True. This would permit the field to automatically increase its height to display the fields' entire contents.

Distribute Space

To help evenly space three or more objects you may choose Format, Horizontal or Vertical Spacing from the menu bar. For two or more objects you may also increase, decrease or remove space from between the objects.

How to Set Tab Order

For a User Form to be truly user-friendly, we must ensure the order of your fields is established by setting the tab order. The user of your User Form should be able to press [Tab] to get to each field in the order the information is required. Assigning the tab order is managed through the TabIndex property in the Properties window. The TabIndex field consists of integers. The first field begins with a TabIndex of 0 up to one less than the total number of TabIndex objects on your User Form. You may also opt to prevent a user from tabbing to a field with a TabIndex by changing the TabStop property to False. Additionally you may have a need to automatically tab after a user key enters information by changing the AutoTab property to True.

Chapter 6:
Code: Inside & Out

Attaching VBA Code

References

Working with Comments

Auto List Members and Auto Quick

User Form Code Structure

Binding Data to User Form

Working with Code

Testing and Debugging the Code

Attaching VBA code

Before you begin coding

The User Form referenced in this book contains Visual Basic for Applications (VBA) code. The intricacies of VBA code are best left for the experienced programmers to explain in other books.

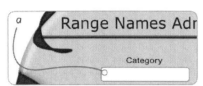

Range Names Admin UserForm

Throughout this book you are introduced to straightforward VBA code with a general description of what you can expect from the code. My experience is that many people can become overwhelmed with trying to understand all of the inner workings of VBA coding. I strongly encourage people who are just beginning to work with VBA code to focus only on the code needed to complete your project and gradually experiment with other code over time. Take it in stride.

You will add your code within the Visual Basic Editor window. The code you use can be added within modules, attached to worksheets, workbooks and objects. To do this you can right click on an item in the Project Explorer window and select View Code. Start typing in your code. It is that simple.

cboCategory: Code

The code attached to this combo box allows the user to choose from a list of range names referenced within this workbook.

Code ComboBox	Resources	
	Referenced By	3
	Private Sub btnAddCat_Click()	
	Private Sub btnDeleteCat_Click()	
	Private Sub UserForm_Initialize()	
	Relies On	1
	Worksheet	fmAdmin

Code: Part 1 of 1

```
Private Sub cboCategory_Change()

'Insert Range Names into the worksheet frmAdmin starting at n1
Worksheets("frmAdmin").Range("n1") = Worksheets("frmAdmin").Range _
("K" & cboCategory.ListIndex + 2)

Worksheets("frmAdmin").Range("o1") = Worksheets("frmAdmin").Range _
("l" & cboCategory.ListIndex + 2)


If Worksheets("frmAdmin").Range("n1") <> "Range" Then

Dim strWkCrit As String
Dim strCrit As String
Dim rTable As Range
Dim ws As Worksheet

strCrit = Range("n1")
strWkCrit = Range("o1")

Set rTable = Range(strCrit)

Worksheets(strWkCrit).Range(strCrit).Sort _
Key1:=Worksheets(strWkCrit).Range(strCrit), _
Order1:=xlAscending, Header:=xlYes, _
Key2:=Worksheets(strWkCrit).Range(strCrit)

Set rTable = rTable.Resize(rTable.Rows.Count - 1).Offset(1)
Me.cboDelete.RowSource = rTable.Address

End If
End Sub
```

NOTE

As you begin to become more familiar with code you will notice there are several ways to take an approach with your code to achieve the same results. The ideal situation is to try and stick with a specific code structure and naming convention.

In this book I have chosen to combine various combinations of code and structure to show how you can take different approaches with coding. Each way is just as effective. You will eventually pick a style that works best for you.

References

Whenever you intend to use code that will specify a specific data management method, or reference objects in another Microsoft application, you must set a reference to the application's type library. For example: if you plan to reference objects through Automation (OLE Automation) in Outlook from within your Excel VBA User Form, you need to select the references within the Visual Basic Editor Window to the Outlook type library. **If you do not, you receive puzzling error messages and then the code you create will not work.**

Very, Very Important: **Avoid frustration! A best practice is to establish all References prior to coding or some of your code references will not work.**

Office Application	Object Library
2003	11.0
2007	12.0
2010	14.0

The reference can be set with the Visual Basic Editor in Excel, or you can set a reference within your code. Keep in mind before you begin any coding you must make sure you have established the References in the VBE environment. If you do not achieve this step prior to coding, you may forget. When it comes time to run your code you may become puzzled when it doesn't work.

Working with References

- Select the check boxes next to the applications type libraries you want to reference.

- By default, a few references will already be selected when you work with a new workbook. Depending on your version of Excel these references could include the following:

  - Visual Basic For Applications

  - Microsoft Excel 11.0 Object Library

  - OLE Automation

  - Microsoft Office 11.0 Object Library

- Previously selected Library types appear at the top of the Reference Dialog box.

- In the Reference Dialog box the Library Types are listed in alphabetical order.

- All of the objects, methods and properties of the referenced application type libraries appear in the Object Browser making it easy to view what properties and methods are available to each object.

How to access the Reference Window

1. Open Excel.

2. Press the [Alt] and [F11] keys simultaneously to open the Visual Basic Editor.

3. Verify the User Form displays in the Object Window to the right of the Visual Basic Editor Window.

NOTE	You can access the References window from any other view. I chose the Object Window view solely because we will begin coding in the next section.

4. Select Tools and References on the menu in the Visual Basic Editor Window.

5. Scroll down the References Dialog box and select the following:

    5.1 Microsoft User Forms 2.0 Object Library from the list.

    5.2 Visual Basic For Applications

    5.3 Microsoft Excel 11.0 Object Library

    5.4 OLE Automation

    5.5 Microsoft Office 11.0 Object Library

6. Click the OK button.

NOTE	References to 11.0 are only needed when working with Office 2003 Applications. Remember to select the correct References when your code references objects in other versions of Office applications. If you are referencing 12.0 objects in your code and you only have 11.0 Reference Library Types selected, you will experience a version issue and receive a compile error when it comes time to run your code.
	Prior to exiting the References Dialog box, always scroll to the top of the list and verify the following Library Types are currently selected. If they are not, scroll through the list and select the needed Library Types. After you make your selections and click the OK button your selections will move to the top of the Reference Window when you open it the next time.

Working with Comments

Comments help to provide a description and intended purpose of the code. The use of comments makes it helpful when it is time to debug your code and maintain and update your code. When collaborating on projects or as a good User Form practice, comments make it easier to remember what you had done at the time when you entered your code a month, or a year later.

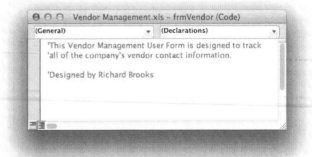

NOTE   Even though I place comments throughout my code, I found it very useful to add
                        project notes within a Module. I place all of my detailed comments in this module
                        such as Revision History, Bugs, Fixes, research notes, detailed issues with resolutions
                        and so forth. This centralized approach is a very valuable resource you can refer to
                        time and time again during the development of your project and when you return at
                        a later time to make modifications to your code.

1. It is best for everyone involved to provide a clear overview of your code and any details of a particular
    tricky piece of code or the technique you used.

2. You may prefer to list any issues you may have discovered during the course of development, or a brief
    history of previously attempted pieces of code and why you may have chosen to change it to the current
    code.

3. The date you created the code, when it was last revised, and any routines it may call are extremely
    beneficial pieces of information and you should include these in your comments. Every little bit helps to
    refresh your memory.

4. Although many people choose to add their code first and then come back later to add their comments
    you may find it most useful to add your comments as you code. The disadvantage to leaving commenting
    of your code until the end is that you may forget to add the comments, or you may have to reexamine
    your code to recall its purpose and in most cases this process could prove to be lengthy and very time
    consuming.

5. Anything after a single quote (') on a line converts everything from that point to the end of the line, to a
    comment. The default font color for lines of comments is green.

6. To prevent bits of code from running during testing, it may be very useful to comment it out. To achieve
    this would normally require you to add a single quote at the beginning of each line of code you do not
    want to run and then deleting each quote after you have completed your testing. For large sections of
    code this process could be very tedious.

    There is a much easier way to comment and uncomment large blocks of code. One of the ways to achieve
    this is as follows:

    6.1   In the Visual Basic Editor window select View, Toolbars, and Customize.

    6.2   Click on the Commands tab and then select the Edit category.

    6.3   Scroll down the list of commands and then select and drag the Comment Block option to your
            standard toolbar. Repeat this step for the Uncomment Block option.

    6.4   Click the Close button.

NOTE   To comment out a line or large sections of code, first highlight the code and then click
                        the Comment Block button on your standard toolbar. To uncomment an area, simply
                        highlight the line or section of code and click the Uncomment Block button.

Auto List Members and Auto Quick

The Visual Basic Editor has some very helpful features, which include pop up listings such as Auto List
Members, and Auto Quick Info. You will come to appreciate the power of these tools. A drop-down list
displays as you type your code to help you complete the spelling of keywords, determine the properties or

methods available for an object. This is a very useful check on your code syntax. By default the Auto List Members and Auto Quick Info options are available.

Working with Auto List Members and Auto Quick

1. If you enter your code and the drop-down list does not appear, try anyone of the following:

    1.1   Verify the Auto List Members and Auto Quick Info options are active. In the Visual Basic Editor window select Tools, and Options from the menu. Click on the Editor tab. Verify the Auto List Members and Auto Quick Info under the Code Settings section are selected and then click the OK button.

    1.2   Check your spelling or your syntax.

User Form Code Structure

Many programmers I have worked with use a very basic code structure when they are developing. I have chosen to take the same approach. The User Form Code Structure referenced in this section is purely a matter of choice on my part. I find it works well for me at the beginning to write on paper the code I plan to utilize in this structured format.

Shared Resources	This code displays at the top and it should contain references you plan to use in multiple places throughout your code.
User Form Initialize	Place code in this section you want to initiate the moment the User Form is activated.
Bind Data	This section contains multiple subroutines you will utilize to bind the data to the User Form fields.
Navigation	This section contains multiple subroutines in reference to the User Form navigation. The code in this section specifies what will result from selecting the left navigation, right navigation buttons.
Manage Data	This section contains multiple subroutines in reference to managing the User Form data. The code in this section specify what will result from selecting the; add, delete, update, and save buttons.
Extras	This section should include the extra features you want to include on your User Form such as any code specific to formatting data, printing records, search options, generating unique record IDs or how to open other applications.

The following sections within this chapter reference the User Form code structure. Comments are used within the Code Window to help you structure your code based on this concept.

Shared Resources

To help us refer to any data during the program execution we will create variables. The process of defining a variable and its data type is called variable declaration. In VBA you can declare variables as either implicit or explicit.

Assigning a value to a variable without declaring it first would be an example of an implicit declaration. This type of approach would make creating procedures very easy, but has the potential to most likely cause errors in your code. Issues tend to result from spelling mistakes or naming-conflict errors. Since the compiler assigns data types to implicit variables there is the potential for assigning of the wrong data type to your variable.

As a good form of practice it is best to use explicit declarations. By using Option Explicit at the beginning of your code you can declare variables for the entire module for which they are used. For example, if we intend for a variable titled intAnswer to contain only integer values we would then declare Dim intAnswer as the Integer at the beginning of our code and then the variable can be used throughout the entire module.

| NOTE | Variable names cannot contain spaces or the %, $, +, -, &, !, #, @, or * symbols. The name must also begin with a letter. |

In this section you will store references to strings, variants, integers and so forth. This code displays after the words Option Explicit and at the top of the code window above all of the other code.

Example:

```
' *******************************************************
' *                 Shared Resources
' *******************************************************
Option Explicit
Public Cancelled As Boolean
Dim vaInfo As Variant
Dim RngData As Range
Dim vaData As Variant
Dim rowcount As Long
Dim intRowCount As Integer
Dim ws As Worksheet
```

Binding Data to a User Form

The purpose of your User Form is usually to bind your data to your data source. Although a User Form can be designed to just display data, a User Form is much more effective if it does not only display your data, but allows you to navigate and modify the data as well. To achieve this we will utilize code to help us bind the data to our User Form.

To ensure you are adding code to the correct object, you want to right-click the object and then select View Code from the shortcut menu. The subroutine automatically adds the beginning and ending tags for the specific object you selected.

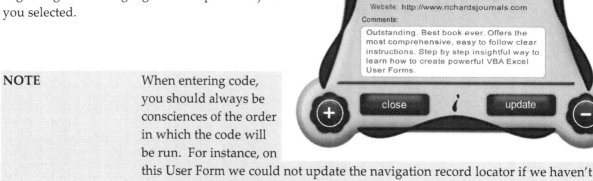

NOTE	When entering code, you should always be consciences of the order in which the code will be run. For instance, on

this User Form we could not update the navigation record locator if we haven't updated the fields it was based on.

Working with code

In this book we take a very straightforward approach with the code. Most of the code referenced in this book includes a comment describing how it works. What you won't find is the in-depth look into the intricacies of

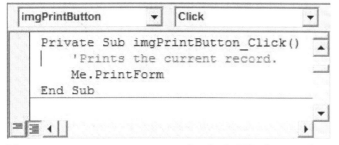

coding and an explanation of the complexity of coding is best left for the more hard core programming authors. What you will discover when you begin to enter the following code is how easy it is and how forgiving the Visual Basic Editor can be for anyone who has no or little knowledge of coding.

There are many ways to access the Code Window in the Visual Basic Editor Window as explained earlier in this book.

1. You can access the code by doing any one of the following.
    1.1. Right-click a User Form in the Project Explorer Window and select View Code from the shortcut menu.
    1.2. Click the View Code button at the top of the Project Explorer Window.
    1.3. Press the [F7] key.

1.4. Right-click the User Form or any object in the Object View Window and select View Code from the shortcut menu.

1.5. Select View and then Code from the menu in the Visual Basic Editor Window.

1.6. Double click on the User Form or any object in the Object View Window.

NOTE   One of the many ways to allow the Visual Basic Editor to automatically create a blank subroutine associated with the corresponding object is to double-click the object. This is a gift and a curse. Sometimes you want a blank subroutine and other times you may not. It is in your best interest to delete any unused blank subroutines to avoid cluttering up the Code Window with unused code.

To view the code without creating a blank subroutine you would right-click a User Form in the Project Explorer Window and then select View Code from the shortcut menu.

2. 2. At the top of the Code Window there are two drop-down lists. Use these drop-down lists to navigate to existing code or to create subroutines associated to a specific object.

2.1. The left drop-down list displays every object on the selected User Form.

2.2. The right drop-down list displays every procedure available for the selected object on the first drop-down list.

NOTE   The method of creating subroutines by selecting from the drop-down list on the right will incorporate the correct code syntax making coding much more accurate and easier for you.

Testing and Debugging the Code

Add Error Handlers

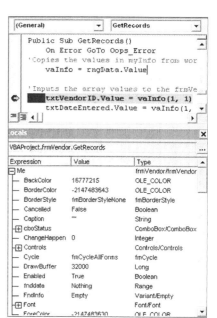

An experienced programmer will tell you that sooner or later you will encounter an error when running your code. Misspelled syntax or references to a keyword typed incorrectly can cause an error that could prevent your procedure from executing properly until it is corrected. Some types of errors can be classified as: compile errors, run-time errors, design and logical errors.

The goal of the error handler is to terminate code execution in a controlled manner. If you do not have error handling code and a run time error occurs, VBA still displays its standard run time error dialog box, which in most cases will be confusing to your User Form users. Creating error handlers allows you to control how an error is handled and what message to display in the event an error occurs. A subroutine can contain multiple error handlers to respond to specific situations.

Example Runtime Error Code

```
Sub MyProject_Macro()
On Error Goto Oops_Error


    'Your code goes here
Exit sub

'Displays a message if an error occurs.
Oops_Error:
    MsgBox Err.Number & " " & Err.Description
End Sub
```

Testing the Code

The execution of code is your opportunity to run your code and perform what is known as a "strength test", "user test" or more commonly called "debugging". Interacting with your code during runtime testing helps you to find and correct any possible errors that may exist within your code. To help track down where in your code the error is located, you may perform your test in Break Mode. This is another option, which exists to help you step through code one command or one procedure at a time as compared to running all the commands at once. Another useful window for testing purposes, which does not display by default but can prove to be a very valuable tool, is the Intermediate window. Typing or dragging lines of code directly into this window prior to including it in your established code affords you the chance to execute the code. This quick test method makes it easier to focus on immediate coding flaws before you move further.

Debugging the Code

Too often programmers become complacent with the fact their code has compiled with no errors. The next and most important step is to begin testing and debugging your code. To help with this process, utilize break points in your lines of code that tells VBA to pause the execution of the line of code where the break point is set, before the code has been executed. By doing this you have placed the code execution in break mode. With break points in place, use the [F8] key to step through code line by code line watching each line of code execute. When VBA code stops at a break point the line becomes highlighted. By pressing [F8] you then execute the highlighted line of code.

To view variables in a procedure and their values executed at a break point, use the valuable tool the Locals Window. With it you can see the value of each variable and where it changes as you step through the code.

Chapter 7:
Step-by-Step

Save As

The .xls file format is compatible with Excel 97 through Excel 2003 for Windows and Excel 98 through Excel 2004 for Mac. Saving in this format will permit you to preserve the Visual Basic Application (VBA) macro code and Excel 4.0 macro sheets needed for creating User Forms. Therefore, when creating any User Form, make sure you save your Microsoft Excel workbook in the format .xls.

Images Available for Download

The background image and the referenced buttons in this chapter are available for download at http://www.RichardsJournals.com.

On our website, locate and then select the Download option on our navigation bar. On the Download page, click on the book title "The Excel VBA User Form Conundrum Solved".

Prior to downloading and using the images please review and abide by the Terms of Use, the Permissions and Trademark guidelines on our site. The option to download the images will appear after you select the "Agree" button.

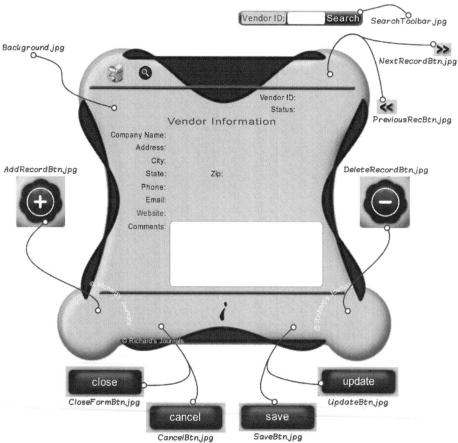

| NOTE | When necessary, refer to the previous chapters for more in depth knowledge on how to perform specific tasks referenced in the following step-by-step instructions. |

Step One: Pre-work

Create Project Overview Checklist

The scenario for this project is that you have been asked to create a Vendor Management User Form to track your company's vendor information. For the sake of time, the Project Overview Checklist in Appendix A has been created for you and is based on this Scenario. Use it for the following steps.

Create the Folder Structure

To store the images and all of the items needed for this project, create a folder titled Vendor Data on your computer and include the folder structure; Code Snippets, Documents, Forms, Images, and Modules as seen below. The location of the main folder can be on the C: drive or on your desktop. The choice is yours.

Create the User Form Images

The rough sketch below is based on the scenario and the project overview checklist in Appendix A. With the rough sketch and the project overview checklist as a guide, open the graphics editor application of your choice and create the images needed for the User Form. Save all the images you create in the images folder.

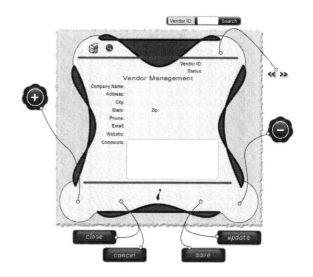

Step Two: Preparing the Workbook

Preparing the workbook sets the foundation for your User Form. The Worksheet tab names, column headers, Workbook name, range names and data will be referenced in your code. To ensure you have covered all needed steps, refer to your checklist frequently.

Create a workbook

NOTE   If you decide to change the name of your Workbook in the future, always remember to update the reference to the workbook name in your code under UserForm Initialize.

1. Open a blank workbook, save as **Vendor Management.xls**. (There is a space between the two words.)

2. Add another worksheet for a total of two worksheets.

3. Rename the Worksheets

    3.1. Rename Sheet1 as VendorData.

    3.2. Rename Sheet2 as Admin.

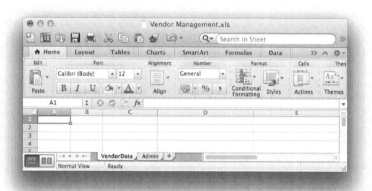

Enter Column Header Names on VendorData Worksheet

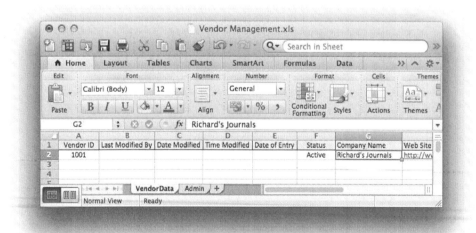

Include spaces in the field names below.

1. On the VendorData Sheet enter the following field names as column headers in the corresponding cells.

Column(s)	Column Header
A1	Vendor ID
B1	Last Modified By
C1	Date Modified
D1	Time Modified
E1	Date of Entry
F1	Status
G1	Company Name
H1	Address
I1	City
J1	State
K1	Zip
L1	Phone
M1	E-mail
N1	Website
O1	Comments

Enter Test Data

Enter the data as displayed including spaces.

1. On the VendorData sheet enter the following data in the corresponding cells. Cells C2, D2 and E2 have been intentionally left blank. These cells will be populated after you begin using the User Form.

Column(s)	Data
A2	1001
B2	AD23112
C2	
D2	
E2	
F2	Active
G2	Richard's Journals

H2	1 MaGlades Dr.
I2	Miami
J2	FL
K2	96722
L2	0005551212
M2	contactus@richardsjournals.com
N2	http://www.richardsjournals.com
O2	Specializes in high quality IT books.

Enter Column Header Names on Admin Worksheet

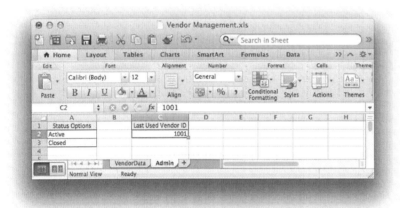

Include spaces in the field names below.

1. On the Admin Sheet enter the following field names in the corresponding cells.

Column(s)	Column Header
A1	Status Options
C1	Last Vendor ID

Enter Admin Data

Enter the data as displayed including spaces.

1. On the Admin sheet enter the following data in the corresponding cells.

Column(s)	Data
A2	Active
A3	Closed
C2	1001

Define Range Name

NOTE Name ranges can be created using this method or you can embed the references into your code.

Create rngStatus Range

1. Select any cell on the Admin worksheet tab.
2. Define a range name
   2.1. Select Insert, Name, and Define from the menu.
   2.2. After the Define window opens, enter in the field Names in the workbook: rngStatus *ok*
   2.3. Enter in the field Refers to: =OFFSET(Admin!$A$1,0,0,COUNTA(Admin!$A:$A),1)
3. Select the Add button.

Create rngVendorID Range

4. Select any cell on the VendorData worksheet tab.
5. Define a range name
   5.1. Select Insert, Name, and Define from the menu.
   5.2. After the Define window opens, enter in the field Names in the workbook: rngVendorID *Member ID*
   5.3. Enter in the field Refers to: =OFFSET(VendorData!$A$1,0,0,COUNTA(VendorData!$A:$A),1)
6. Select the Add button. *Member-Date   MemberData*

Create rngVendorInfo Range

7. Select any cell on the VendorData worksheet tab.
8. Define a range name
   8.1. Select Insert, Name, and Define from the menu.
   8.2. After the Define window opens, enter in the field Names in the workbook: rngVendorInfo *MemberInfo*
   8.3. Enter in the field Refers to: =OFFSET(VendorData!$A$1,0,0,COUNTA(VendorData!$A:$A),15)
9. Select the Add button. *MemberData   31*

Create rngVendorInfoTmp Range

The rngVendorInfoTmp range will be defined within the imgAddRecordBtn code, which is referenced, later in this chapter. The range will display within the Define Name window after the UserForm is run for the first time and the user selects the Add Record button.

```
'Resize the iRowCount and rename rngVendorInfoTmp
.Resize(iRowCount).Name = "rngVendorInfoTmp"
```

Step Three: Inserting Objects

NOTE	If you choose not to utilize images, refer to the "**Workaround Steps**" in the Appendix section of this book.

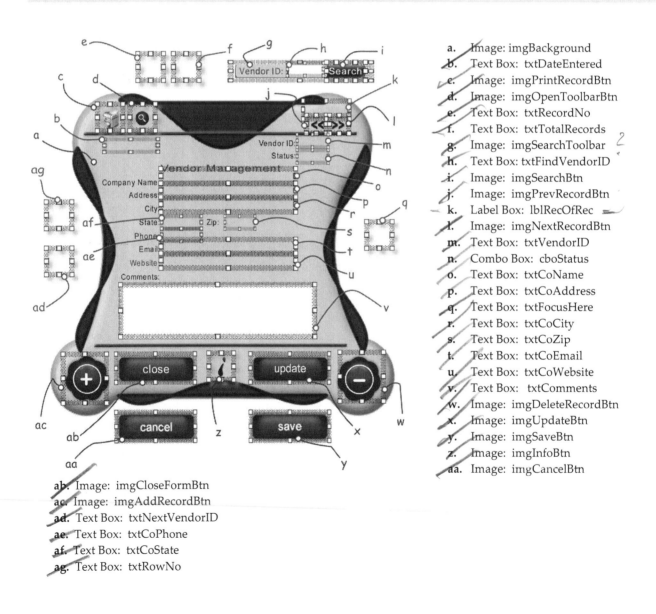

a. Image: imgBackground
b. Text Box: txtDateEntered
c. Image: imgPrintRecordBtn
d. Image: imgOpenToolbarBtn
e. Text Box: txtRecordNo
f. Text Box: txtTotalRecords
g. Image: imgSearchToolbar
h. Text Box: txtFindVendorID
i. Image: imgSearchBtn
j. Image: imgPrevRecordBtn
k. Label Box: lblRecOfRec
l. Image: imgNextRecordBtn
m. Text Box: txtVendorID
n. Combo Box: cboStatus
o. Text Box: txtCoName
p. Text Box: txtCoAddress
q. Text Box: txtFocusHere
r. Text Box: txtCoCity
s. Text Box: txtCoZip
t. Text Box: txtCoEmail
u. Text Box: txtCoWebsite
v. Text Box: txtComments
w. Image: imgDeleteRecordBtn
x. Image: imgUpdateBtn
y. Image: imgSaveBtn
z. Image: imgInfoBtn
aa. Image: imgCancelBtn

ab. Image: imgCloseFormBtn
ac. Image: imgAddRecordBtn
ad. Text Box: txtNextVendorID
ae. Text Box: txtCoPhone
af. Text Box: txtCoState
ag. Text Box: txtRowNo

Next Steps

Adding the User Form background image is the first step in layering objects to create the User Form look. **We will begin by adding all of the Objects to your User Form. Then you will add the code.**

Object Properties Specifications

- A properties Spec page has been created for each object referenced on the previous page. At the top of each column there is an image identifying the corresponding letter followed by the name of the object.

- A Step-by-Step section identifies the type of object you will add to the User Form. Below this section are the property references you will change for this object. All remaining property values not referenced will keep their default value.

- Helpful relevant notes will be listed under the Notes section.

- A brief outline of actions that are performed based on the type of Action identified. The type of action could be specific to an On Click, After Update or On Open event, to name a few.

- You are encouraged to refer to the exploded image on the previous page as a reference point for positioning the objects on your User Form.

Example: What to do next

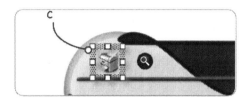

imgPrintRecordBtn

Clicking on this print icon will print the User Form with the current record.

Step-by-Step: Adding Transparent Image Object

1. Select the Image object from the Toolbox Toolbar.
2. Then click any where on the background.
3. Verify the newly added object is selected and then make changes in the Properties Window as outlined below.

Property	Value
(Name)	imgPrintRecordBtn
BackStyle	0-fmBackStyleTransparent
BorderStyle	0-fmBorderStyleNone
ControlTipText	Print Current Record
*Height	20
*Left	56
MouseIcon	Icon
MousePointer	99-fmMousePointerCustom
*Top	44
*Width	20

Notes:

This image is part of the background image. To create a button you place a transparent Image Object over the printer icon.

Actions: On click

- Prints the current viewable record and the User Form.

Procedures: How to add Objects

The following steps are a detail outline of the procedures you will follow for each of the referenced objects on the next several pages.

- Select and view the recently created User Form.
- Double-click on the frmVendor User Form located in the Object Window on the left side of screen or right click on frmVendor and select View Object.
- Open the Toolbox toolbar by selecting View, and then Toolbox from the menu bar.
- For each of the following referenced objects, select the corresponding object from the Toolbox Toolbar and then click any where on the background image. At this point the location doesn't matter, because you will soon reposition each newly added object by modifying the properties.
- Verify the newly added object is selected and then make the referenced changes in the Properties Window for each of the following objects. One the attributes that require a change to the properties are referenced.
- Save after each property is updated.

NOTE	The image objects referenced over the next several pages are either a transparent image with no picture or it will refer to an existing picture identified on the Picture property field.

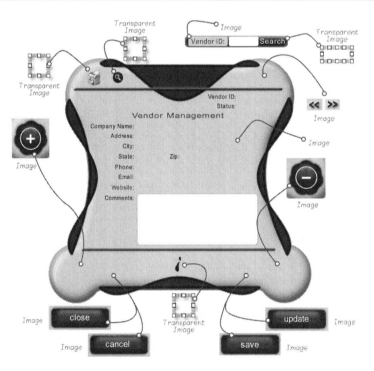

Let's begin

Now it is time to create the User Form and add the objects. Refer to and follow the step-by-step instructions and update the properties for each referenced object on the next several pages.

User Form Properties

frmVendor	
All referenced objects will be layered onto this User Form.	

Step-by-Step: Adding User Form

1. Verify Vendor Management.xls file is open.
2. Open Visual Basic Editor by pressing the [Alt] and [F11] keys simultaneously.
3. In the Visual Basic Editor window select **Insert**, and **User Form** from the menu.
4. On the left side of the window, click on the User Form in the Object Window to select it.
5. Once the User Form is selected make the following changes to the User Form in the Properties Window.

(Name)	frmVendor
BackColor	&H00FFFFFF&
BackStyle	0 - fmBackStyleTransparent
BorderStyle	0 - fmBorderStyleNone
Caption	(Press the spacebar once)
*Height	394.5
KeepScrollBarsVisible	0 - fmScrollBarsNone
*Left	0
*Top	4.5
*Width	364.5

Notes:

The User Form is considered the canvas where all of the objects will reside.

Actions: On Open

- Hides the Vendor Management.xls workbook.
- Locks txtDateEntered and txtVendorID fields to prevent manual changes.
- Resize the User Form canvas to fit the exact dimensions of the User Form.
- Set the font name, size, back style, border style and special effect for all Text Box objects on the User Form.
- Populates the cboStatus Combo Box list.
- Sets the ChangeHappen variable to 0.
- Sets the focus to the hidden txtFocusHere field. This prevents the user from accidently updating a field in error.
- Resizes the txtFocusHere field and locks the field.
- Retrieves data from the workbook and populates the User Form fields.

Very Important

* All referenced objects in this book will be repositioned on the User Form by modifying the object properties. This method is much more accurate than moving the object manually. The Height, Left, Top and Width attributes in the Properties window for all objects referenced in this chapter are approximations only. You will have to make adjustments as needed to accurately reposition your objects over your background image.

** Referenced images identified in the Pictures attribute for an object, in this Chapter are not included and the assumption is you created them previously for this project.

*** When selecting 99-fmMousePointerCustom for the MousePointer attribute, the next step is to select the MouseIcon. You can select any cursor icon available on your computer. Usually this is located under C:\Windows\Cursors\. The extension is .cur. A choice in this book is to use a mouse pointer that resembles a hand pointing. The choice is yours.

Object Properties

imgBackground	txtDateEntered
All other objects will be layered over this background image.	The date the record was created. Through the use of code this information is automatically populated on the workbook.

Step-by-Step: Adding Image Object	**Step-by-Step: Adding Text Box Object**
1. Select the Image object from the Toolbox Toolbar.	1. Select the Text Box object from the Toolbox Toolbar.
2. Then click any where on the background.	2. Then click any where on the background.
3. Verify the newly added object is selected and then make changes in the Properties Window as outlined below.	3. Verify the newly added object is selected and then make changes in the Properties Window as outlined below.

imgBackground properties:

(Name)	imgBackground
BackColor	&H00FFFFFF&
BackStyle	0-fmBackStyleTransparent
BorderStyle	0-fmBorderStyleNone
*Height	324
*Left	0
**Picture	Background.jpg
*Top	24
*Width	360

txtDateEntered properties:

(Name)	txtDateEntered
BackStyle	0-fmBackStyleTransparent
BorderStyle	0-fmBorderStyleNone
*Height	13
*Left	54
SpecialEffect	0-fmSpecialEffectFlat
*Top	72
*Width	60

Notes:	Notes:
Remember all height, left, top and width positions and dimensions are approximations. Adjust the position of your background image as needed to accommodate all of the other objects.	This object is a Text Box and is locked down to prevent manual modifications to the data.

Actions:	Actions: Add New Record
None	• Changes to any record will not have an impact to the date in this field. It is only populated the first time a new record is created.

Object Properties (continued)

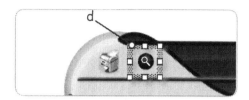

imgPrintRecordBtn	imgOpenToolbarBtn
Clicking on the print icon prints the User Form with the current record.	Clicking on the icon opens or closes the Search Toolbar.

Step-by-Step: Adding Transparent Image Object	**Step-by-Step: Adding Transparent Image Object**
1. Select the Image object from the Toolbox Toolbar.	1. Select the Image object from the Toolbox Toolbar.
2. Then click any where on the background.	2. Then click any where on the background.
3. Verify the newly added object is selected and then make changes in the Properties Window as outlined below.	3. Verify the newly added object is selected and then make changes in the Properties Window as outlined below.

Properties **C** Image	(Name)		imgPrintRecordBtn
	BackStyle		0-fmBackStyleTransparent
	BorderStyle		0-fmBorderStyleNone
	ControlTipText		Print Current Record
	*Height		20
	*Left		56
	***MouseIcon		Icon
	MousePointer	99-fmMousePointerCustom	
	*Top		44
	*Width		20

Properties **d** Image	(Name)		imgOpenToolbarBtn
	BackStyle		0-fmBackStyleTransparent
	BorderStyle		0-fmBorderStyleNone
	ControlTipText		Open Search Toolbar
	*Height		12
	*Left		92
	***MouseIcon		Icon
	MousePointer	99-fmMousePointerCustom	
	*Top		48
	*Width		12

Notes:	Notes:
This image is part of the background image. To create a button you place a transparent Image Object over the printer icon.	This image is part of the background image. To create a button you place a transparent Image Object over the Open Search Toolbar icon.

Actions: On click	Actions: On click
• Prints the current viewable record and the User Form.	• Clicking once on the icon will display the Search Toolbar. • Clicking on the icon again will hide the Search Toolbar.

Object Properties (continued)

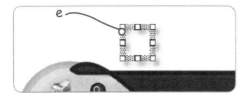

txtRecordNo		txtTotalRecords	
Identifies the current record position within the data range.		Identifies the total number of records in the data range.	

Step-by-Step: Adding Text Box Object		**Step-by-Step: Adding Text Box Object**	
1. Select the Text Box object from the Toolbox Toolbar. 2. Then click any where on the background. 3. Verify the newly added object is selected and then make changes in the Properties Window as outlined below.		1. Select the Text Box object from the Toolbox Toolbar. 2. Then click any where on the background. 3. Verify the newly added object is selected and then make changes in the Properties Window as outlined below.	

Properties *e* Text Box	(Name)	txtRecordNo	Properties *f* Text Box	(Name)	txtTotalRecords
	BorderStyle	0-fmBorderStyleNone		BorderStyle	0-fmBorderStyleNone
	*Height	13		*Height	13
	*Left	120		*Left	168
	*Top	12		*Top	12
	Visible	False		Visible	False
	*Width	30		*Width	30

Notes:		**Notes:**	
This is a hidden field on the User Form.		This is a hidden field on the User Form.	

Actions: On User Form open and after update		**Actions: On User Form open and after update**	
• This field always displays the current record position within the data range when the User Form opens and navigating through the records on the User Form.		• This field always displays the total number of records in the data range. • The number in this field updates when a new record is added or deleted.	

Object Properties (continued)

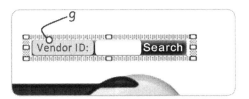

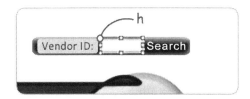

imgSearchToolbar	txtFindVendorID
Entering a Vendor ID on the Search Toolbar and then clicking on the Search button displays the record matching the search criteria.	The Vendor ID you are searching is entered into this field.

Step-by-Step: Adding Image Object	Step-by-Step: Adding Text Box Object
1. Select the Image object from the Toolbox Toolbar.	1. Select the Text Box object from the Toolbox Toolbar.
2. Then click any where on the background.	2. Then click any where on the background.
3. Verify the newly added object is selected and then make changes in the Properties Window as outlined below.	3. Verify the newly added object is selected and then make changes in the Properties Window as outlined below.

imgSearchToolbar properties (Properties g — Image)

Property	Value
(Name)	imgSearchToolbar
BackStyle	0-fmBackStyleTransparent
BorderStyle	0-fmBorderStyleNone
*Height	19.45
*Left	210
**Picture	SearchToolbar.jpg
*Top	0
Visible	False
*Width	138

txtFindVendorID properties (Properties h — Text Box)

Property	Value
(Name)	txtFindVendorID
BackStyle	0-fmBackStyleTransparent
BorderStyle	0-fmBorderStyleNone
*Height	13
*Left	270
SpecialEffect	0-fmSpecialEffectFlat
*Top	2
Visible	False
*Width	34

Notes:

imgSearchToolbar	txtFindVendorID
The search toolbar will display or be hidden when the Open Search Toolbar button is selected.	The txtFindVendorID is only visible when the Search Toolbar is open.

Vendor ID: Search

Actions: On open | **Actions: On change**

Actions: On open	Actions: On change
• When the toolbar opens, two other objects will also display on the toolbar. The txtFindVendorID and the imgSearchBtn.	• Since the Vendor ID is 1 to 4 characters in length, this field is limited to four characters. • Only numbers are accepted in this field.

Object Properties (continued)

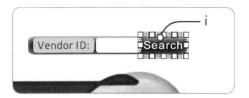

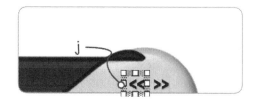

imgSearchBtn	imgPrevRecordBtn
After entering a Vendor ID on the Search Toolbar and then clicking on the Search button displays the record matching the search criteria.	Clicking on this button navigates you to the previous record on the User Form.

Step-by-Step: Adding Transparent Image Object	Step-by-Step: Adding Image Object
1. Select the Image object from the Toolbox Toolbar.	1. Select the Image object from the Toolbox Toolbar.
2. Then click any where on the background.	2. Then click any where on the background.
3. Verify the newly added object is selected and then make changes in the Properties Window as outlined below.	3. Verify the newly added object is selected and then make changes in the Properties Window as outlined below.

(Name)	imgSearchBtn	(Name)	imgPrevRecordBtn
BackStyle	0-fmBackStyleTransparent	BackStyle	0-fmBackStyleTransparent
BorderStyle	0-fmBorderStyleNone	BorderStyle	0-fmBorderStyleNone
ControlTipText	Search for Vendor ID	ControlTipText	View Previous Record
*Height	14	*Height	18
*Left	312	*Left	270
***MouseIcon	Icon	***MouseIcon	Icon
MousePointer	99-fmMousePointerCustom	MousePointer	99-fmMousePointerCustom
*Top	0	Picture	PrevRecordBtn.jpg
Visible	False	*Top	51
*Width	36	*Width	24

Notes:	Notes:
This image is part of the Search Toolbar image. To create a button you place a transparent Image Object over the search text on the toolbar.	The image is designed to blend with the User Form background image. Through the use of code you will be able to hide or display the image based on the user's actions.

Actions: On click	Actions: On click
• If the txtFindVendorID field is blank then display a message.	• Checks if the variable ChangeHappen equals 1, indicating the current record has been modified. If the user modifies the current record and then decides to click on the previous record button, they will receive the following yes or no prompt.
• If the entered Vendor ID in the txtFindVendorID is valid then display the record on the User Form, else display an error message.	"You have made a change to this record. Do you wish to update the record?"
• After the Search button is clicked, then clear the txtFindVendorID field.	• Determines if you are viewing the first. If so, a message will display notifying the user they are on the first.
• Update the Record of Records label with the displayed record.	
• If you locate a record in a closed status, the fields are locked due to the DisableObjects subroutine.	

Object Properties (continued)

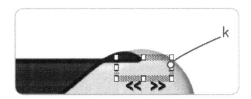

lblRecOfRec	imgNextRecordBtn
Displays the record number of total records based on the current view.	Clicking on this button navigates you to the next record on the User Form.

Step-by-Step: Adding Label Object	Step-by-Step: Adding Image Object
1. Select the Label object from the Toolbox Toolbar.	1. Select the Image object from the Toolbox Toolbar.
2. Then click any where on the background.	2. Then click any where on the background.
3. Verify the newly added object is selected and then make changes in the Properties Window as outlined below.	3. Verify the newly added object is selected and then make changes in the Properties Window as outlined below.

Properties k Label

(Name)	lblRecOfRec
BackStyle	0-fmBackStyleTransparent
BorderStyle	0-fmBorderStyleNone
*Height	12
*Left	264
SpecialEffect	0-fmSpecialEffectFlat
TextAlign	2-fmTextAlignCenter
*Top	42
*Width	54

Properties I Image

(Name)	imgNextRecordBtn
BackStyle	0-fmBackStyleTransparent
BorderStyle	0-fmBorderStyleNone
*Height	18
*Left	294
***MouseIcon	Icon
MousePointer	99-fmMousePointerCustom
Picture	NextRecordBtn.jpg
*Top	51
Width	24

Notes:

1. If the record is in a closed status all of the fields are disabled, because of the Call DisableObjects subroutine referenced in the User Form initialize section of code.

Notes:

The image is designed to blend with the User Form background image. Through the use of code you will be able to hide or display the image based on the user's actions.

>>

Actions: After update

- If the txtFindVendorID field is blank then display a message.
- If the entered Vendor ID in the txtFindVendorID is valid then display record on the User Form, else display a message.
- After the Search button is clicked, then clear the txtFindVendorID field.
- Display the Record of Records label with the displayed record.

Actions: On click and after update

- Checks if the variable ChangeHappen equals 1, indicating the current record has been modified. If the user modifies the current record and then decides to click on the next record button, they will receive the following yes or no prompt.

  "You have made a change to this record. Do you wish to update the record?"

- Determines if you are viewing the last record. If so, a message will display notifying the user they are on the last record.

Object Properties (continued)

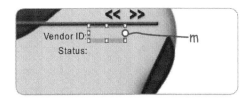 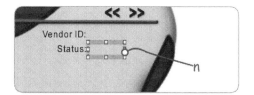

txtVendorID	cboStatus
Displays a uniquely generated ID.	Displays an active or closed status from the drop down list.
Step-by-Step: Adding Text Box Object	**Step-by-Step: Adding Combo Box Object**
1. Select the Text Box object from the Toolbox Toolbar. 2. Then click any where on the background. 3. Verify the newly added object is selected and then make changes in the Properties Window as outlined below.	1. Select the Combo Box object from the Toolbox Toolbar. 2. Then click any where on the background. 3. Verify the newly added object is selected and then make changes in the Properties Window as outlined below.

txtVendorID properties:

(Name)	txtVendorID
BackStyle	0-fmBackStyleTransparent
BorderStyle	0-fmBorderStyleNone
*Height	13
*Left	258
SpecialEffect	0-fmSpecialEffectFlat
*Top	68
*Width	42

cboStatus properties:

(Name)	cboStatus
BackStyle	0-fmBackStyleTransparent
*Height	13
*Left	258
ShowDropButtonWhen	1-fmShowDropButtonWhenFocus
SpecialEffect	0-fmSpecialEffectFlat
TabIndex	1
*Top	84
*Width	60

Notes:

txtVendorID:
1. The GenUniqueNum subroutine is used to automatically generate a unique ID. The ID is based on the maximum ID last used plus 1.
2. The visible property for this field is set to false. It is hidden when the User Form is open.

cboStatus:
Based on the cboStatus_Change event, if the cboStatus field displays a closed status all of the fields on the User Form will be locked.

Actions: On add new record and delete record
- Adding a new record will automatically assign a unique id to the newly added record.
- A deleted ID will never be regenerated.

Actions: On change
- The cboStatus list is automatically populated when the User Form opens.
- The list is based on the rngStatus.
- After updating the field the ChangeHappen variable will be set to 1.

Object Properties (continued)

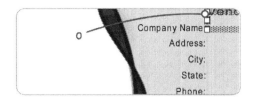

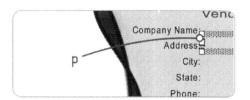

txtCoName			txtCoAddress		
Enter the Vendor company name.			Enter the Vendor company address.		
Step-by-Step: Adding Text Box Object			**Step-by-Step: Adding Text Box Object**		
1. Select the Text Box object from the Toolbox Toolbar.			1. Select the Text Box object from the Toolbox Toolbar.		
2. Then click any where on the background.			2. Then click any where on the background.		
3. Verify the newly added object is selected and then make changes in the Properties Window as outlined below.			3. Verify the newly added object is selected and then make changes in the Properties Window as outlined below.		

	(Name)	txtCoName		(Name)	txtCoAddress
	BackStyle	0-fmBackStyleTransparent		**BackStyle**	0-fmBackStyleTransparent
	BorderStyle	0-fmBorderStyleNone		**BorderStyle**	0-fmBorderStyleNone
	*Height	13		***Height**	13
	*Left	120		***Left**	120
	SpecialEffect	0-fmSpecialEffectFlat		**SpecialEffect**	0-fmSpecialEffectFlat
	TabIndex	2		**TabIndex**	3
	*Top	108		***Top**	121
	*Width	132		***Width**	132

Notes:	**Notes:**
None	None.
Actions: After update	**Actions: After update**
• After updating the field the ChangeHappen variable will be set to 1.	• After updating the field the ChangeHappen variable will be set to 1.

Object Properties (continued)

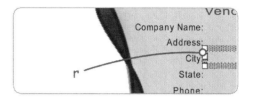

txtFocusHere		txtCoCity	
A hidden field used to temporarily capture the cursor.		Enter the Vendor company city.	
Step-by-Step: Adding Text Box Object		**Step-by-Step: Adding Text Box Object**	
1. Select the Text Box object from the Toolbox Toolbar. 2. Then click any where on the background. 3. Verify the newly added object is selected and then make changes in the Properties Window as outlined below.		1. Select the Text Box object from the Toolbox Toolbar. 2. Then click any where on the background. 3. Verify the newly added object is selected and then make changes in the Properties Window as outlined below.	

Properties q **Text Box**	(Name)	txtFocusHere
	BackStyle	0-fmBorderStyleNone
	*Height	13
	*Left	312
	*Top	156
	*Width	30

Properties r **Text Box**	(Name)	txtCoCity
	BackStyle	0-fmBackStyleTransparent
	BorderStyle	0-fmBorderStyleNone
	*Height	13
	*Left	120
	SpecialEffect	0-fmSpecialEffectFlat
	TabIndex	4
	*Top	132
	*Width	114

Notes:	Notes:
1. By redirecting the position of the cursor on the User Form, helps to establish if a change was made to a field and prevents the user from accidently modifying a field when navigating between records. 2. When the User Form opens, the Height and Wdith are readjusted to 0 for each. The field is also locked to prevent modifications.	None

Actions: After update	**Actions: After update**
• Based on certain actions from the user, the cursor is set to this field, including when the User Form opens.	• After updating the field the ChangeHappen variable will be set to 1.

Object Properties (continued)

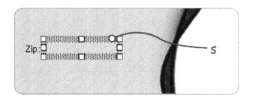

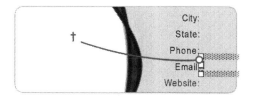

txtCoZip		**txtCoEmail**	
Enter the Vendor company zip code.		Enter the Vendor company email address.	

Step-by-Step: Adding Text Box Object	**Step-by-Step: Adding Text Box Object**
1. Select the Text Box object from the Toolbox Toolbar.	1. Select the Text Box object from the Toolbox Toolbar.
2. Then click any where on the background.	2. Then click any where on the background.
3. Verify the newly added object is selected and then make changes in the Properties Window as outlined below.	3. Verify the newly added object is selected and then make changes in the Properties Window as outlined below.

	(Name)	txtCoZip		(Name)	txtCoEmail
	BackStyle	0-fmBackStyleTransparent		**BackStyle**	0-fmBackStyleTransparent
	BorderStyle	0-fmBorderStyleNone		**BorderStyle**	0-fmBorderStyleNone
	***Height**	13		***Height**	13
	***Left**	182		***Left**	120
	SpecialEffect	0-fmSpecialEffectFlat		**SpecialEffect**	0-fmSpecialEffectFlat
	TabIndex	6		**TabIndex**	8
	***Top**	148		***Top**	174
	***Width**	66		***Width**	156

Notes:	**Notes:**
You can either enter in a zip code or zip code plus four. Either is acceptable.	1. The mail to, cc, subject, and body of the email that are automatically populated when you double click on a valid email address in this field are editable within the code.
	2. Depending on your email application settings, after you double click on the email address, your email may open and maximize on your screen or default to your task bar at the bottom of the screen.

Actions: On change and after update	**Actions: On double click or after update**
• After updating the field the ChangeHappen variable will be set to 1.	• After updating the field the ChangeHappen variable will be set to 1.
• This field is limited to ten characters. This includes the zip code plus four and the hyphen character.	• Double clicking on a valid email address will open your email application and automatically populate the mail to, cc, subject and body of the email with data from the record in view.
• Only a hyphen and numbers are accepted in this field.	• If you attempt to double click on this field and there is no email address you will receive an error message.

Object Properties (continued)

txtCoWebsite	txtComments
Enter the Vendor company web site.	Enter any comments applicable to this company.

Step-by-Step: Adding Text Box Object	**Step-by-Step: Adding Text Box Object**
1. Select the Text Box object from the Toolbox Toolbar. 2. Then click any where on the background. 3. Verify the newly added object is selected and then make changes in the Properties Window as outlined below.	1. Select the Text Box object from the Toolbox Toolbar. 2. Then click any where on the background. 3. Verify the newly added object is selected and then make changes in the Properties Window as outlined below.

Properties **u** Text Box			Properties **v** Text Box		
	(Name)	txtCoWebsite		(Name)	txtComments
	BackStyle	0-fmBackStyleTransparent		BackStyle	0-fmBackStyleTransparent
	BorderStyle	0-fmBorderStyleNone		BorderStyle	0-fmBorderStyleNone
	*Height	13		*Height	64
	*Left	120		*Left	126
	SpecialEffect	0-fmSpecialEffectFlat		MultiLine	True
	TabIndex	9		SpecialEffect	0-fmSpecialEffectFlat
	*Top	187		TabIndex	10
	*Width	168		*Top	202
				*Width	156

Notes:	**Notes:**
None.	If the comments you enter exceed the size of the comments field, a vertical scroll bar will display.

Actions: On change and double click	**Actions: On change**
• After updating the field the ChangeHappen variable will be set to 1. • Double clicking on a valid URL (web site) address will open the referenced web site. • If you attempt to double click on this field and there is no URL (web site) address you will receive an error message.	• Entering comments that exceed the width of this field will automatically wrap to the next line.

Object Properties (continued)

imgDeleteRecordBtn	imgUpdateBtn
Clicking on this button will delete the current record.	Clicking on this button will update any changes to the current record.

Step-by-Step: Adding Image Object	Step-by-Step: Adding Image Object
1. Select the Image object from the Toolbox Toolbar. 2. Then click any where on the background. 3. Verify the newly added object is selected and then make changes in the Properties Window as outlined below.	1. Select the Image object from the Toolbox Toolbar. 2. Then click any where on the background. 3. Verify the newly added object is selected and then make changes in the Properties Window as outlined below.

imgDeleteRecordBtn properties:

Property	Value
(Name)	imgDeleteRecordBtn
BackStyle	0-fmBackStyleTransparent
BorderStyle	0-fmBorderStyleNone
Caption	Delete Current Record
*Height	54
*Left	292
***MouseIcon	Icon
MousePointer	99-fmMousePointerCustom
**Picture	DeleteRecordBtn.jpg
*Top	282
*Width	54

imgUpdateBtn properties:

Property	Value
(Name)	imgUpdateBtn
BackStyle	0-fmBackStyleTransparent
BorderStyle	0-fmBorderStyleNone
*Height	30
*Left	198
***MouseIcon	Icon
MousePointer	99-fmMousePointerCustom
**Picture	UpdateBtn.jpg
*Top	282
*Width	78

Notes:

imgDeleteRecordBtn	imgUpdateBtn
1. A minimum of one record is required to be maintained within the workbook. Therefore any attempt to delete the last record in the workbook will result in an error message. 2. The image is designed to blend with the User Form background image. Through the use of code you will be able to hide or display the image based on the user's actions.	By default this button displays on the User Form when it is open. Clicking on the Add New Record button will cause this button's title to change to the word "save". After the new record is added or the user decides not to add a new record, the button title will revert back to the word "update".

Actions: On click

imgDeleteRecordBtn	imgUpdateBtn
• If you click on the button a yes or no prompt will display verifying your intent to delete this record.	• Updates the workbook with any changes to the current record. • After updating the field the ChangeHappen variable will be set to 0.

Object Properties (continued)

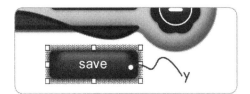

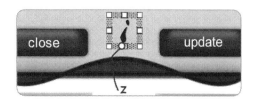

imgSaveBtn		imgInfoBtn	
Clicking on this button will save a newly added record.		Clicking on this button will open the User Guide document.	

Step-by-Step: Adding Image Object		**Step-by-Step: Adding Transparent Image Object**	
1.	Select the Image object from the Toolbox Toolbar.	1.	Select the Image object from the Toolbox Toolbar.
2.	Then click any where on the background.	2.	Then click any where on the background.
3.	Verify the newly added object is selected and then make changes in the Properties Window as outlined below.	3.	Verify the newly added object is selected and then make changes in the Properties Window as outlined below.

(Name)	imgSaveBtn		(Name)	imgInfoBtn
BackStyle	0-fmBackStyleTransparent		**BackStyle**	0-fmBackStyleTransparent
BorderStyle	0-fmBorderStyleNone		**BorderStyle**	0-fmBorderStyleNone
*Height	30		**ControlTipText**	View Info
*Left	198		*Height	24
***MouseIcon	Icon		*Left	171
MousePointer	99-fmMousePointerCustom		***MouseIcon	Icon
**Picture	SaveBtn.jpg		**MousePointer**	99-fmMousePointerCustom
*Top	342		*Top	282
Visible	False		*Width	12
*Width	78			

Notes:	Notes:
By default this button does not display on the User Form when it is open. Clicking on the Add New Record button will cause the Update button's title to change to the word "save". After the new record is added or the user decides not to add a new record, the button title will revert back to the word "update".	1. You can update the original code to open any document. However, the code associated with this button is currently designed to open a document titled Vendor Management User Guide.doc located in the same folder as the Vendor Management.xls workbook.
	2. The User Guide content is located in Appendix B of this book.
	3. This image is part of the background image. To create a button you place a transparent Image Object over the icon.

Actions: On click	Actions: On click
• Updates the workbook with the new record and ID.	• Opens a Microsoft Word document titled "Vendor Management User Guide.doc".
• Sets the ChangeHappen variable to 0.	
• The imgCancelBtn, and imgSaveBtn visible property is set too false.	The code provides two different options for the path of the document associated with this button.
• The imgPrevRecordBtn, imgNextRecordBtn, imgCloseFormBtn, lblRecOfRec, imgUpdateBtn, imgAddRecordBtn, and imgDeleteRecordBtn visible property is set to true.	• Option 1 will allow you to specify a specific path for your document. Option 1 is commented out by default.
• The User Form displays the newly added record and the lblRecOfRec field is updated.	• Option 2 will assume your document is located in the same folder as your Vendor Management.xls workbook. Option 2 is currently the default code.
• The cursor is moved to the txtFocusHere field.	

Object Properties (continued)

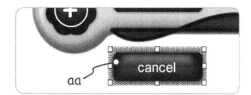
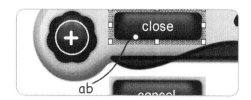

imgCancelBtn	imgCloseFormBtn
Clicking on this button will cancel the option to add a new record.	Clicking on this button will close the User Form.

Step-by-Step: Adding Image Object	Step-by-Step: Adding Image Object
1. Select the Image object from the Toolbox Toolbar.	1. Select the Image object from the Toolbox Toolbar.
2. Then click any where on the background.	2. Then click any where on the background.
3. Verify the newly added object is selected and then make changes in the Properties Window as outlined below.	3. Verify the newly added object is selected and then make changes in the Properties Window as outlined below.

Left column — imgCancelBtn properties:

(Name)	imgCancelBtn
BackStyle	0-fmBackStyleTransparent
BorderStyle	0-fmBorderStyleNone
*Height	30
*Left	84
***MouseIcon	Icon
MousePointer	99-fmMousePointerCustom
**Picture	CancelBtn.jpg
*Top	342
Visible	False
*Width	78

Right column — imgCloseFormBtn properties:

(Name)	imgCloseFormBtn
BackStyle	0-fmBackStyleTransparent
BorderStyle	0-fmBorderStyleNone
*Height	30
*Left	84
***MouseIcon	Icon
MousePointer	99-fmMousePointerCustom
**Picture	CloseFormBtn.jpg
*Top	282
*Width	78

Notes:

Left (imgCancelBtn):

1. By default this button does not display on the User Form when it is open. Clicking on the Add New Record button will cause the Close button's title to change to the word "cancel". After the new record is added or the user decides not to add a new record, the button title will revert back to the word "close".

2. The image is designed to blend with the User Form background image. Through the use of code you will be able to hide or display the image based on the user's actions.

Right (imgCloseFormBtn):

1. By default this button displays on the User Form when it is open. Clicking on the Add New Record button will cause the Close button's title to change to the word "cancel". After the new record is added or the user decides not to add a new record, the button title will revert back to the word "close".

2. The image is designed to blend with the User Form background image. Through the use of code you will be able to hide or display the image based on the user's actions.

Actions: On click

Left (imgCancelBtn):

- Prior to canceling the new entry, a yes or no prompt will appear.

- Sets the ChangeHappen variable to 0.

- The imgCancelBtn, and imgSaveBtn visible property is set too false.

- The imgPrevRecordBtn, imgNextRecordBtn, imgCloseFormBtn, lblRecOfRec, imgUpdateBtn, imgAddRecordBtn, and imgDeleteRecordBtn visible property is set to true.

- The User Form returns back to the previously view record.

- The cursor is moved to the txtFocusHere field.

Right (imgCloseFormBtn):

- Closes the User Form and saves all recent changes.

Object Properties (continued)

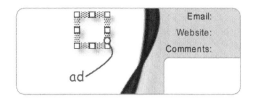

imgAddRecordBtn		txtNextVendorID	
Clicking on this button will permit you to add a new record.		Displays the next available Vendor ID.	

Step-by-Step: Adding Image Object		**Step-by-Step: Adding Text Box Object**	
1. Select the Image object from the Toolbox Toolbar.		1. Select the Text Box object from the Toolbox Toolbar.	
2. Then click any where on the background.		2. Then click any where on the background.	
3. Verify the newly added object is selected and then make changes in the Properties Window as outlined below.		3. Verify the newly added object is selected and then make changes in the Properties Window as outlined below.	

Properties / ac / Image

(Name)	imgAddRecordBtn
BackStyle	0-fmBackStyleTransparent
BorderStyle	0-fmBorderStyleNone
***Height**	72
***Left**	2.5
****MouseIcon**	Icon
MousePointer	99-fmMousePointerCustom
****Picture**	AddRecordBtn.jpg
***Top**	276.5
***Width**	66

Properties / ad / Text Box

(Name)	txtNextVendorID
BorderStyle	0-fmBorderStyleNone
***Height**	13
***Left**	12
***Top**	198
Visible	False
***Width**	30

Notes:

1. The image is designed to blend with the User Form background image. Through the use of code you will be able to hide or display the image based on the user's actions.

2. By default this button displays on the User Form when it is open. Clicking on the Add New Record button will set its visible property to false. This is to prevent the user from clicking on the button again until they decide to save or cancel.

Notes:

The visible property for this field is set to false. It is hidden when the User Form is open.

Actions: On Click

- The imgCancelBtn, and imgSaveBtn visible property is set too true. Both are also repositioned on the User Form.

- The imgPrevRecordBtn, imgNextRecordBtn, imgCloseFormBtn, lblRecOfRec, imgUpdateBtn, imgAddRecordBtn, and imgDeleteRecordBtn visible property is set to false.

- All of the fields are cleared to allow the addition of the new record data.

Actions: On Open and after change

- The field will display the next available vendor id based on the data in cell c2 on the Admin worksheet.

Object Properties (continued)

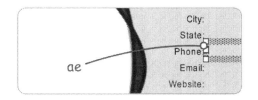
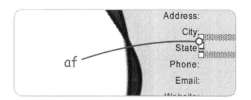

txtCoPhone	txtCoState
Enter the Vendor company phone number.	Enter the Vendor company state location.

Step-by-Step: Adding Text Box Object	**Step-by-Step: Adding Text Box Object**
1. Select the Text Box object from the Toolbox Toolbar. 2. Then click any where on the background. 3. Verify the newly added object is selected and then make changes in the Properties Window as outlined below.	1. Select the Text Box object from the Toolbox Toolbar. 2. Then click any where on the background. 3. Verify the newly added object is selected and then make changes in the Properties Window as outlined below.

(Name)	txtCoPhone	(Name)	txtCoState
BackStyle	0-fmBackStyleTransparent	**BackStyle**	0-fmBackStyleTransparent
BorderStyle	0-fmBorderStyleNone	**BorderStyle**	0-fmBorderStyleNone
*Height	13	***Height**	13
*Left	120	***Left**	120
SpecialEffect	0-fmSpecialEffectFlat	**SpecialEffect**	0-fmSpecialEffectFlat
TabIndex	7	**TabIndex**	5
*Top	162	***Top**	146
*Width	72	***Width**	42

Notes:	Notes:
Although the User Form will display the phone number with parenthesis and a hyphen the phone number entered into this field will be stored with the numbers only in the workbook. Example: (000)555-1212 will be stored as 0005551212 in the workbook.	None

Actions: On change	Actions: On change
• Maximum character length accepted is 13. • Automatically displays the parenthesis and hyphen as the phone number is entered. • Limited to numbers only.	• Limited to only two characters.

Object Properties (continued)

txtRowNo	
Displays the current row number in the workbook of the current record in view.	

Step-by-Step: Adding Text Box Object	

1. Select the Text Box object from the Toolbox Toolbar.
2. Then click any where on the background.
3. Verify the newly added object is selected and then make changes in the Properties Window as outlined below.

(Name)	txtRowNo
BorderStyle	0-fmBorderStyleNone
***Height**	13
***Left**	12
SpecialEffect	0-fmSpecialEffectFlat
***Top**	138
Visible	False
***Width**	30

Notes:
The visible property for this field is set to false. It is hidden when the User Form is open.

Actions: On change
• The field automatically updates with the current row number when the user advances to the next or previous record.

Step Four: Attach Code

I encourage you to apply the principals for testing and debugging as referenced in the section Testing and Debugging the Code. When possible, it is best to test sections of your code as you go. This approach helps you to identify possible issues with your code before proceeding on to the next piece of code. For helpful code hints, refer to the Attach VBA section in this book.

Very, Very Important: Avoid frustration! A best practice is to establish all References prior to coding or some of your code references will not work.

Office Application	Object Library
2003	11.0
2007	12.0
2010	14.0

Add References

1. Open the Vendor Management.xls workbook.

2. Press the [Alt] and [F11] keys simultaneously to open the Visual Basic Editor.

3. Verify the User Form displays in the Object Window to the right of the Visual Basic Editor Window.

4. Select Tools and References on the menu in the Visual Basic Editor Window.

5. Scroll down the References Dialog box and select the following:

    5.1 Microsoft User Forms 2.0 Object Library from the list.

    5.2 Visual Basic For Applications

    5.3 Microsoft Excel 11.0 Object Library

    5.4 OLE Automation

    5.5 Microsoft Office 11.0 Object Library

6. Click the OK button.

7. Save.

Running Code

Normally you are encouraged to test your code as you go. This is useful when you are creating your own project and you are unsure of how your code will work. Since the code for this project has been previously tested, we recommend you run the code after all of the code has been entered at the end of Step Four.

NOTE

1. To run the code you can press the [F5] key, select Run, and then Run Macro from the menu bar or select the Run Sub/UserForm option on the toolbar within the VBE Window.
2. To stop the code from running, click on the VBE window and select the Reset button on the toolbar.

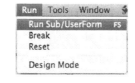

This Workbook Code

Verify the "Vendor Management.xls" workbook is open.

1. Open the Visual Basic Editor by selecting the [Alt] and [F11] keys simultaneously.

2. Right click on ThisWork in the Project Window under the Microsoft Excel Objects section.

3. Then select View Code from the shortcut menu.

4. Enter the following code.

Very Important: Make it easy! The Workbook_Open and Workbook_BeforeClose code hides the Workbook and automatically opens your User Form. Therefore making it difficult for you to troubleshoot issues or to quickly navigate between the workbook and the Visual Basic Editor Window. To avoid this frustration, temporarily comment out the following code when you are testing your User

Form. Then uncomment it after you are satisfied with the performance of the User Form.

```
Private Sub Workbook_Open()
'Automatically display the User Form when Excel opens.
    frmVendor.Show
End Sub


Private Sub Workbook_BeforeClose(Cancel As Boolean)
'Ensure the Excel application is visible prior to closing.
    Application.Visible = True
End Sub
```

User Form and Object Code

IMPORTANT   SAVE TIME

For the first go around, you can choose to exclude all comments and enter only the actual code. Remember the comments begin with a single quote and are illustrated in green font. The comments are intended to give you some insight to how the code will work and are not required for the User Form to work correctly.

Let's Begin: Insert Code

Verify the "Vendor Management.xls" workbook is open.

1. Open the Visual Basic Editor by selecting the [Alt] and [F11] keys simultaneously.

2. Right click on the frmVendor User Form in the Project Window and then select View Code from the shortcut menu.

3. Enter the following code.

4. After entering the code for each object, select Save from the menu bar and continue until you have entered all of the code.

VERY IMPORTANT

1. The success of your project relies heavily on the accuracy of the code you enter. Misspellings, extra spaces, wrong code structure or incorrect references can contribute to your code not working properly. Give extra care to the details of the code referenced in this section.

   Each section identifies the title of the referenced code and should not be included when you enter your code. The code you will enter is in small font.

2. If at any point after you enter the code, you close out of the Vendor Management.xls workbook and then reopen it, a prompt will display with the options to Enable Macros, Do Not Open, and Disable Macros. To run the User Form, always select Enable Macros. To prevent the User Form from automatically opening, you can select Disable Macros. This will open the Workbook and then you can make your necessary changes or continue adding your code.

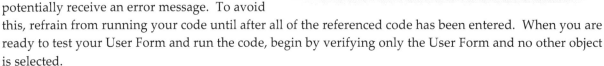

3. Keep in mind that some of the code referenced is dependent on other pieces of code. Therefore, if you attempt to run your code prior to entering all of the code, you could potentially receive an error message. To avoid this, refrain from running your code until after all of the referenced code has been entered. When you are ready to test your User Form and run the code, begin by verifying only the User Form and no other object is selected.

   a. Remember, to run your code, press the [F5] key or select Run Sub/UserForm on the toolbar in the VBE window.

   b. To stop the code from running, select the Reset button on the toolbar.

Enter User Form_Initialize and User Form_QueryClose Code

```
Option Explicit

Public Cancelled As Boolean

Dim vaInfo As Variant
Dim FndInfo As Variant
Dim UCInfo(1 To 15) As Variant
Dim rngData As Range
Dim fnddata As Range
Dim UCdata As Range
Dim iRowCount As Integer

Public ChangeHappen As Integer

Public Sub UserForm_Initialize()
    On Error GoTo Oops_Error

    'Hide any changes taking place in the background.
    Application.ScreenUpdating = False
```

```
'Hide Excel Workbook application.
Application.Visible = False

'Since these two fields are automatically populated it is best to lock
'them to prevent someone from accidentally modifying the data.
Me.txtDateEntered.Locked = True
Me.txtVendorID.Locked = True
```

Member ID

```
'Chose not to set the focus to the field txtCoName to prevent someone from
'accidentally deleting or modifying the name in error.

'Sets the User Form size when it opens.
Me.Height = 384
Me.Width = 370

'Centers the User Form on your screen.
Me.StartUpPosition = "2"

'Required to ensure the correct workbook is active, in case the user has multiple
'Excel workbooks open.

'Make sure you change the name of the workbook referenced below
'when you change the name of the workbook or else you may receive the error message
'9 Subscript out of range.
Workbooks("Vendor Management.xls").Activate

'You may discover a quark in the VBE window when you are modifying the Font, Font
'Style and Font Size.  Sometimes the Font attributes you identified will be
'correct when the user is viewing the User Form and sometimes the system defaults to
'something different. It is frustrating.

'To prevent this from happening I chose to loop through each Text Box object and
'set the Font properties one time when the User Form initializes.  This ensures you
'get a specific cosmetic look on the User Form.

Dim cTxtCont As Control
For Each cTxtCont In Me.Controls
    If TypeName(cTxtCont) = "TextBox" Then
        cTxtCont.Font.Name = "Arial"
        cTxtCont.Font.Size = 8
        cTxtCont.BackStyle = fmBackStyleTransparent
        cTxtCont.BorderStyle = fmBorderStyleNone
        cTxtCont.SpecialEffect = fmSpecialEffectFlat
    End If
Next cTxtCont

'This is a "Nice to know!" piece of code.  You can Use this code to modify image
'objects BackStyle and BorderStyle properties when the User Form initializes.
'There is no need for this code here because we have chosen to modify our image
'objects during the design phase.

'To use it for another project all you have to do is uncomment it by removing the
'single quote apostrophe (') from the beginning of the next six lines of code.
'Dim cImgCont As Control
'For Each cImgCont In Me.Controls
'If TypeName(cImgCont) = "Image" Then
'cImgCont.BackStyle = fmBackStyleTransparent
'cImgCont.BorderStyle = fmBorderStyleNone
'End If
'Next cImgCont

'Modifies the Combo Box cboStatus fields Font properties. For the
'purpose of demonstrating how you can make those changes also directly in the
'Properties window, I chose not to include modify the BackStyle, BorderStyle and
'other attributes here. However, you can choose to make those changes here.
```

```vba
    With Me.cboStatus
        .Font.Name = "Arial"
        .Font.Size = 8
    End With


    Dim irng As Range

    'Demonstrates how to reference a defined range minus the column
    'header.
    With Worksheets("Admin")
        Set irng = .Range("rngStatus")

        'Important Note: Do not reference the RowSource for a combobox list. Instead use
        '.List and reference the .Value like the following example.
        cboStatus.List = irng.Resize(irng.Rows.Count - 1).Offset(1).Value
    End With

    'We need to select the worksheet to ensure the data collected from the User Form
    'is entered within your data list.
    Worksheets("VendorData").Select

    'This code loads the data you have previously entered onto your User Form.
    LoadData 2


    'Establish what record will display when the User Form opens.
    With Range("rngVendorInfo")
        Set rngData = .Rows(2)
        Call GetRecords
    End With


    'Set the txtFocusHere dimensions and lock the field to prevent changes to the field.
    With Me.txtFocusHere
        .Width = 0
        .Height = 0
        .Locked = True
    End With


    'Calls the NavRec subroutine that will populate the "records of records" label on
    'the User Form.
    NavRec

    'The following 2 lines of code will prevent a prompt from displaying should the
    'user choose to immediately navigate to the next record after the User Form opens.
    ChangeHappen = 0
    Me.txtFocusHere.SetFocus
    'MsgBox ChangeHappen


    Exit Sub

    'Displays a message if an error occurs.
Oops_Error:
    MsgBox Err.Number & " " & Err.Description

End Sub



Private Sub UserForm_QueryClose(Cancel As Integer, CloseMode As Integer)
    On Error GoTo Oops_Error

    'Prevents the user from selecting the "x" in the upper right corner of the
```

```
    'form to close the form.
    If CloseMode = vbFormControlMenu Then
        MsgBox "Please use the Close button on the form to close this form.  Thank you."
        Cancel = True
    End If

    Exit Sub

    'Displays a message if an error occurs.
Oops_Error:
    MsgBox Err.Number & " " & Err.Description

End Sub
```

✓ Enter imgSearchBtn Code

cmdOpenMemberInfo   *cmdSearch*

```
Private Sub imgSearchBtn_Click()
    On Error GoTo Oops_Error

    Dim rngData As Range

    If Me.txtFindVendorID = "" Then
        MsgBox "Please enter a Vendor ID number."

    Else

        On Error GoTo SayWhat
        Sheets("VendorData").Select
        Set rngData = Worksheets("VendorData").Range("rngVendorInfo")
        With rngData.Find(txtFindVendorID.Value, lookat:=xlWhole)
            txtRowNo.Value = .Row
        End With

        Worksheets("VendorData").Select

        With Range("rngVendorInfo")
            NewLoadData frmVendor.txtRowNo
            Set fnddata = Range("rngVendorInfo").Rows(txtRowNo)
            Call RecordFound
        End With
    End If

    Me.txtFindVendorID = ""

    Call NavRec

    Exit Sub

SayWhat:
    MsgBox Me.txtFindVendorID & " is not a valid Vendor ID number.  Please try again."

    Exit Sub
Oops_Error:
    MsgBox Err.Number & " " & Err.Description

End Sub
```

Enter imgPrintRecordBtn Code

```
Private Sub imgPrintRecordBtn_Click()
    On Error GoTo Oops_Error
    'Prints the current record.
    Me.PrintForm
    Exit Sub

    'Displays a message if an error occurs.
Oops_Error:
    MsgBox Err.Number & " " & Err.Description

End Sub
```

Enter imgOpenToolbarBtn Code

```
Private Sub imgOpenToolbarBtn_Click()
    On Error GoTo Oops_Error

'The following code checks if the Search Toolbar is
'already open.  Then it hides and displays the
'toolbar accordingly. It also sets the focus to the txtFindVendorID field.
    If Me.imgSearchToolbar.Visible = False Then
        Me.imgSearchToolbar.Visible = True
        Me.imgSearchBtn.Visible = True
        Me.txtFindVendorID.Visible = True
        Me.txtFindVendorID.Value = ""
        Me.txtFindVendorID.SetFocus
    Else
        Me.imgSearchToolbar.Visible = False
        Me.imgSearchBtn.Visible = False
        Me.txtFindVendorID.Visible = False
    End If
    Exit Sub

    'Displays a message if an error occurs.
Oops_Error:
    MsgBox Err.Number & " " & Err.Description

End Sub
```

Enter imgPrevRecordBtn Code

```
Private Sub imgPrevRecordBtn_Click()
    On Error GoTo Oops_Error

    Me.txtFocusHere.SetFocus

    Call CheckForChange

    'The assumption is if the user makes changes to
    'the data on the Form and then clicks on the
    'previous or next record button they must have intended
    'to save the changes.  Therefore a prompt will
    'appear.
```

```
    'Identifies the current record location within
    'the data list.
    Set rngData = Range("rngVendorInfo").Rows(txtRowNo)

    'Determines if this is the first or last record
    'in your data list.
    If rngData.Row > Range("rngVendorInfo").Rows(2).Row Then
        LoadData frmVendor.txtRowNo - 1
        Set rngData = Range("rngVendorInfo").Rows(txtRowNo.Value)
        Call GetRecords
        Call DisableObjects

    Else

        'This code is used to let the user know they are viewing the first record.
        MsgBox "You have reached the first record."

    End If

    Dim iRowCount As Integer

    'This is used to display the total rows in the range minus the header.
    With Range("rngVendorInfo")
        iRowCount = .Rows.Count
        Me.txtTotalRecords = iRowCount - 1
        NavRec
    End With

    ChangeHappen = 0

    Exit Sub

    'Displays a message if an error occurs.
Oops_Error:
    MsgBox Err.Number & " " & Err.Description

End Sub
```

✓ Enter imgNextRecordBtn Code

```
Private Sub imgNextRecordBtn_Click()
    On Error GoTo Oops_Error

    Me.txtFocusHere.SetFocus

    Call CheckForChange

    'Determines if this is the last record and if
    'not move to the next record.
    Set rngData = Range("rngVendorInfo").Rows(txtRowNo)
    If rngData.Row < Range("rngVendorInfo").Rows.Count Then
        LoadData frmVendor.txtRowNo + 1
        Set rngData = Range("rngVendorInfo").Rows(txtRowNo.Value)
        Call GetRecords
        Call DisableObjects
    Else
        'Lets the user know they are viewing the last record.
        'This code is to help handle when the user attempts to go past
        'the last record.
        MsgBox "You have reached the last record."
    End If
```

```
        Dim iRowCount As Integer

        'Displays the total rows in the range minus the header.
        With Range("rngVendorInfo")
            iRowCount = .Rows.Count
            Me.txtTotalRecords = iRowCount - 1

            'Updates the Record of Record field on the User Form.
            NavRec
        End With

        ChangeHappen = 0

        'Displays a message if an error occurs.
        Exit Sub
    Oops_Error:
        MsgBox Err.Number & " " & Err.Description

    End Sub
```

✓ Enter imgAddRecordBtn

```
    Private Sub imgAddRecordBtn_Click()
        On Error GoTo Oops_Error

        'If the user already clicked on the Add Record
        'button and then attempts to click on it
        'again a 'message will display.
        If Me.imgAddRecordBtn.Enabled = False Then

        'Type the following two lines on the same line
            MsgBox "You can not add another record until you cancel or save this record."

        End If

        'After the user chooses to add a new record,
        'it is necessary to disable and hide buttons
        'and fields to prevent the user from making other
        'changes until they decide to save or cancel.
        Me.txtCoName.SetFocus
        Me.imgCancelBtn.Visible = True
        Me.imgSaveBtn.Visible = True
        Me.imgPrevRecordBtn.Visible = False
        Me.imgNextRecordBtn.Visible = False
        Me.lblRecOfRec.Visible = False
        Me.imgCloseFormBtn.Visible = False
        Me.imgUpdateBtn.Visible = False

        'Reposition the Save button onto the User Form.
        With Me.imgSaveBtn
            .Left = 198
            .Top = 282
        End With

        'Reposition the Cancel button onto the User Form.
        With Me.imgCancelBtn
            .Left = 84
            .Top = 282
        End With

        Dim iRowCount As Integer
```

```
With Range ("rngVendorInfo")
    'With the Range of rngVendorInfo set the iRowCount variable
    'equal to the count of rows plus one.
    iRowCount = .Rows.Count + 1

    'Resize the iRowCount and rename rngVendorInfoTmp
    .Resize(iRowCount).Name = "rngVendorInfoTmp"

    'Set the txtRowNo value equal to the iRowCount
    txtRowNo.Value = iRowCount    'new code

    Set rngData = Range("rngVendorInfoTmp").Rows(iRowCount)
    Call GetRecords

    iRowCount = .Rows.Count
    Me.txtTotalRecords = iRowCount - 1

    'Updates the Record of Record field on the User Form.
    Call NavRec

End With

Call NavRec

'Obtain the next available Vendor ID.
Call GenUniqueNum

Sheets("VendorData").Select

'Establishes the default for the Date of Entry, and the Status fields.
Call MyFormDefaults

Me.imgAddRecordBtn.Visible = False
Me.imgDeleteRecordBtn.Visible = False

Exit Sub

'Displays a message if an error occurs.
Oops_Error:
    MsgBox Err.Number & " " & Err.Description

End Sub
```

Enter imgDeleteRecordBtn Code

```
Private Sub imgDeleteRecordBtn_Click()
    On Error GoTo Oops_Error

    Dim iRowCount As Integer
    Dim strAnswer As String

    With Range("rngVendorInfo")
        iRowCount = .Rows.Count    '- 1
        If Range("rngVendorInfo").Rows.Count = 2 Then

            'A minimum of one record is required
            'in your User Form.

            MsgBox "You cannot delete every record"

        Else
```

```
                        'If there is more than one record in the
                        'table then the user will receive the
                        'following message to make sure their
                        'intent is to delete the current record.
                        If Range("rngVendorInfo").Rows.Count > 2 Then

                        'Type the following two lines on the same line.
                            strAnswer = MsgBox("Are you sure you want to delete this record?",
vbQuestion + vbYesNo, "Delete File?")

                            'If the user selects "Yes" then delete the current record.
                            If strAnswer = vbYes Then

                                Set rngData = rngData.Offset(1)
                                rngData.Offset(-1).Delete Shift:=xlUp

                                txtRowNo.Value = iRowCount
                                Set rngData = rngData.Offset(1)
                                LoadData frmVendor.txtRowNo - 1

                                Set rngData = Range("rngVendorInfo").Rows(txtRowNo.Value)

                                Call GetRecords
                                Call NavRec


                                Exit Sub

                                'Do not delete, then exit.
                                If strAnswer = vbNo Then

                                    Exit Sub

                                End If
                            End If
                        End If
                End If
            End With

            With Range("rngVendorInfo")
                iRowCount = .Rows.Count
                Me.txtTotalRecords = iRowCount - 1
            End With

            Exit Sub

            'Displays a message if an error occurs.
Oops_Error:
            MsgBox Err.Number & " " & Err.Description

End Sub
```

Enter imgCloseFormBtn Code

```
Private Sub imgCloseFormBtn_Click()
    On Error GoTo Oops_Error

    AddToWorkbook

    Unload Me
```

```
    'The following 2 lines of code ensure Excel.exe shuts down and closes.
    Application.Quit
    ThisWorkbook.Close SaveChanges:=True

    'For testing purpose, uncomment the following code.
    'This will allow the Excel workbook to remain open in the background.
    'Application.Visible = True

    Exit Sub

    'Displays a message if an error occurs.
Oops_Error:
    MsgBox Err.Number & " " & Err.Description
End Sub
```

Enter imgInfoBtn Code

```
Private Sub imgInfoBtn_Click()

    Dim wdApp As Word.Application
    Dim wdDoc As Word.Document
    Dim myPath As String

    On Error Resume Next
    'Handles Run-time error 429: ActiveX component can't create object.
    'This issue can result for various reasons.

    Set wdApp = GetObject(, "Word.Application")

    'Word isn't already running
    If Err.Number <> 0 Then

        Set wdApp = CreateObject("Word.Application")

    End If

    '0 referenced in the following code is the number zero
    On Error GoTo 0

    'The document referenced in this code is based on the Usrer Guide in
    'Appendix B of this book. Technically you can open any document with the title
    'Vendor Management User Guide.doc.  Remember to change the referenced document name
    'in the code if you decide to change the name of your document.
    'Set this code to point directly to the path and document you have created.

    'Option 1:  This method allows you to refer to a specific path.
    'Set wdDoc = wdApp.Documents.Open("G:\Book July 2009\Vendor Management
    'User Guide.doc")

    'Option 2: This method allows you to specify a relative path to your workbook.
    'This option would require you maintain the Vendor Management User Guide.doc
    'within the same folder as your workbook.
    myPath = ActiveWorkbook.Path & "\Vendor Management User Guide.doc"
    Set wdDoc = wdApp.Documents.Open(myPath)

    wdApp.Visible = True
    wdDoc.Activate

    Exit Sub

End Sub
```

Enter imgCancelBtn Code

```
Private Sub imgCancelBtn_Click()
    On Error GoTo Oops_Error

    Dim Answer As String
    Dim MyNote As String

    MyNote = "Are you sure you want to cancel this entry?"

    'Verify if the user intended to cancel
    'the newly added record.
    Answer = MsgBox(MyNote, vbQuestion + vbYesNo, "???")

    'If the answer is "no", then return to
    'newly added record.
    If Answer = vbNo Then

        ChangeHappen = 0
        Me.txtCoName.SetFocus

        Exit Sub

    Else

        'If the answer is "yes", then remove the newly added record.
        Erase vaInfo

        Worksheets("VendorData").Select

        'Verifies the record the user was last viewing prior to adding a new record.
        Set rngData = Range("rngVendorInfo").Rows(txtRecordNo)
        If rngData.Row < Range("rngVendorInfo").Rows(2).Row Then

            'This code loads the data you have previously entered onto your User Form.
            LoadData 2

            'We establish what record will display when the User Form opens.
            With Range("rngVendorInfo")
                Set rngData = .Rows(2)
                Call GetRecords
            End With

            Me.txtFocusHere.SetFocus
            ChangeHappen = 0

            NavRec

            GoTo SkipToHere

        Else

            LoadData frmVendor.txtRecordNo + 1
            Set rngData = Range("rngVendorInfo").Rows(txtRecordNo.Value + 1)
            Call GetRecords

            Me.txtFocusHere.SetFocus
            ChangeHappen = 0

            'Disable and hide buttons and fields to prevent the user from
            'making other changes until they decide to save or cancel.
SkipToHere:
            Me.imgCancelBtn.Visible = False
```

```
            Me.imgPrevRecordBtn.Visible = True
            Me.imgNextRecordBtn.Visible = True
            Me.lblRecOfRec.Visible = True
            Me.imgAddRecordBtn.Visible = True
            Me.imgDeleteRecordBtn.Visible = True
            Me.imgCloseFormBtn.Visible = True
            Me.imgSaveBtn.Visible = False
            Me.imgUpdateBtn.Visible = True

            ChangeHappen = 0

        End If
    End If
    Exit Sub

    'Displays a message if an error occurs.
Oops_Error:
    MsgBox Err.Number & " " & Err.Description

End Sub
```

Enter imgUpdateBtn

```
Private Sub imgUpdateBtn_Click()
    On Error GoTo Oops_Error

    Call UpdateChanges

    Worksheets("VendorData").Select
    NewLoadData frmVendor.txtRowNo.Value

    'Update the Workbook with the newly added data.
    With Range("rngVendorInfo")
        Set UCdata = Range("rngVendorInfo").Rows(txtRowNo)
        UCdata.Value = UCInfo
    End With

    Me.txtFocusHere.SetFocus
    ChangeHappen = 0

    Exit Sub

    'Displays a message if an error occurs.
Oops_Error:
    MsgBox Err.Number & " " & Err.Description

End Sub
```

✓ Enter imgSaveBtn

```vba
Private Sub imgSaveBtn_Click()
    On Error GoTo Oops_Error

    Me.txtFocusHere.SetFocus

    ChangeHappen = 0

    Call CheckForChange

    Call AddToWorkbook

    MsgBox "New record has been saved."

    Me.imgCancelBtn.Visible = False
    Me.imgSaveBtn.Visible = False
    Me.imgPrevRecordBtn.Visible = True
    Me.imgNextRecordBtn.Visible = True
    Me.imgCloseFormBtn.Visible = True
    Me.lblRecOfRec.Visible = True
    Me.imgUpdateBtn.Visible = True
    Me.imgAddRecordBtn.Visible = True
    Me.imgDeleteRecordBtn.Visible = True

    frmVendor.lblRecOfRec.Caption = frmVendor.txtRecordNo.Value & "  of  " & _
frmVendor.txtTotalRecords.Value + 1

    Exit Sub

    'Displays a message if an error occurs.
Oops_Error:
    MsgBox Err.Number & " " & Err.Description

End Sub
```

✓ Enter txtFindVendorID Text Box Code

```vba
Private Sub txtFindVendorID_Change()
    On Error GoTo Oops_Error

    With Me.txtFindVendorID

        ' maximum acceptable length of a Vendor ID.
        .MaxLength = 4
        .Text = Format(OnlyNumbers(.Text))
    End With

    Exit Sub

    'Displays a message if an error occurs.
Oops_Error:
    MsgBox Err.Number & " " & Err.Description

End Sub
```

Enter cboStatus Combo Box Code

```
Private Sub cboStatus_Change()
    On Error GoTo Oops_Error

    'We call the subroutine DisbaleObjects
    'to ensure the record is locked if the
    'status is changed to "Close".
    Call DisableObjects
    Exit Sub

    'Displays a message if an error occurs.
Oops_Error:
    MsgBox Err.Number & " " & Err.Description

End Sub
```

Enter txtCoZip Code

```
Private Sub txtCoZip_Change()
    With Me.txtCoZip
        .MaxLength = 10
    End With
End Sub

Private Sub txtCoZip_KeyPress(ByVal KeyAscii As MSForms.ReturnInteger)
'Restrict input to numbers only and the hyphen character

'The following code is designed to allow input of
'the Zip plus four which accounts for the usage of
'the hyphen character.
'Therefore only numeric and the hyphen character are
'accepted in this field.
'If you decided not to utilize Zip plus four in this field and instead would prefer
'just the regular zip code then you could choose to use the IsNumeric function.
    Select Case KeyAscii
    Case 8      ' backspace/delete
        ' always allow this key
    Case 45     'hyphen and minus
        ' allow this character
    Case 48 To 57    ' Asc("0") to Asc("9")
        ' allow these characters
    Case Else
        ' reject these characters
        KeyAscii = 0
    End Select

End Sub
```

✓ Enter txtCoPhone Text Box Code

```vba
Private Sub txtCoPhone_Change()
    On Error GoTo Oops_Error

    Dim Phone As String
    Dim Length As Integer

    Phone = txtCoPhone.Text
    Length = Len(Phone)

    With Me.txtCoPhone
        .MaxLength = 13
        'End With

        Select Case Length
        Case 1
            .Text = Format(OnlyNumbers(.Text), "(0")
        Case 4
            .Text = Format(OnlyNumbers(.Text), "(000") & ") "
        Case 9
            .Text = Format(OnlyNumbers(.Text), "(000)000") & "-"
        End Select

    End With

    Exit Sub

    'Displays a message if an error occurs.
Oops_Error:
    MsgBox Err.Number & " " & Err.Description

End Sub


Function OnlyNumbers(inputString As String) As String

    Dim i As Long

    For i = 1 To Len(inputString)
        If Mid(inputString, i, 1) Like "[0-9]" Then
            OnlyNumbers = OnlyNumbers & Mid(inputString, i, 1)
        End If

    Next i

End Function
```

✓ Enter txtCoEmail Text Box Code

```vba
Private Sub txtCoEmail_DblClick(ByVal Cancel As MSForms.ReturnBoolean)
    On Error GoTo Oops_Error

    Dim strLink As String
    If txtCoEmail <> IsNull(txtCoEmail) Then
        On Error GoTo NoCanDo

        'To have a carriage return in the body of
        'the email utilize "%0A" with quotes.
        'The 0 in "%0A% is a zero.
```

```
'Important Note:
'To break long lines of code, you can
'use the &_ to proceed with the code onto the next
'line.   So therefore continue the code below on the
'same line until you come across the & _ and then continue to the next line.

'Each line ending with & _ permits the code to continue to the next
'line. For example the first line of code below starts with strLink
'and ends with & _ on the second line where you would then press your
'Return button to begin the next line of code.  Breaking the line of
'code prior to the & _ characters would cause an error when you attempt
'to run your code.

strLink = "mailto: " & txtCoEmail & "?cc=" & "john.doe@abc123.com" & _
    "&subject=" & txtCoName & "&body=" & txtCoName & _
    "%0A" & txtCoAddress & "%0A" & txtCoCity & ", " & txtCoState & "  " & _
    txtCoZip & "%0A" & txtCoPhone & "%0A" & "%0A" & "%0A" & "%0A" & _
    "We appreciate your business. Please verify " & txtCoPhone & _
    " is the correct phone number for your company. " & _
    "%0A" & "%0A" & "Thank you, " & "%0A" & "%0A" & "Richard's Journals"

    ActiveWorkbook.FollowHyperlink Address:=strLink, NewWindow:=True

Else: Exit Sub

End If
Exit Sub

NoCanDo:
    MsgBox "Field is blank. There is no email address."

    Exit Sub

'Displays a message if an error occurs.
Oops_Error:
    MsgBox Err.Number & " " & Err.Description

End Sub
```

Enter txtCoWebsite Text Box Code

```
Private Sub txtCoWebsite_DblClick(ByVal Cancel As MSForms.ReturnBoolean)
    On Error GoTo Oops_Error

    'Allows the user to double click on a URL to view the page.
    Dim strLink As String

    If txtCoWebsite <> IsNull(txtCoWebsite) Then

        strLink = txtCoWebsite

        ActiveWorkbook.FollowHyperlink Address:=strLink, NewWindow:=True

    End If
    Exit Sub

NoCanDo:
    MsgBox "Field is blank. There is no URL to open."

    Exit Sub
```

```vba
    'Displays a message if an error occurs.
Oops_Error:
    MsgBox Err.Number & " " & Err.Description

End Sub
```

Enter Common User Form Code

```vba
Public Sub MyFormDefaults()
    On Error GoTo Oops_Error

    'This code is a nice to have. It allows you to incorporate a specific format for
    'the Vendor ID numbers on this form by proceeding them with VID and a hyphen (-).
    'Me.txtVendorID.Value = "VID-" & Worksheets("Admin").Range("e2")

    'Stores the next unique Vendor ID
    Me.txtNextVendorID.Value = Worksheets("Admin").Range("e2")

    'Sets the txtVendorID field to the txtNextVendorID field.
    Me.txtVendorID = Me.txtNextVendorID

    'Sets the txtDateEntered field to today's computer date.
    Me.txtDateEntered = Date

    'Set's the default text to the cboStatus field to "Active"
    Me.cboStatus = "Active"

    Exit Sub

    'Displays a message if an error occurs.
Oops_Error:
    MsgBox Err.Number & " " & Err.Description

End Sub


'The manipulation of the ChangeHappen variable helps to
'track if there was a change to the User Form data.
Private Sub cboStatus_AfterUpdate()
    ChangeHappen = 1
End Sub

Private Sub txtCoAddress_AfterUpdate()
    ChangeHappen = 1
End Sub

Private Sub txtCoCity_AfterUpdate()
    ChangeHappen = 1
End Sub

Private Sub txtCoEmail_AfterUpdate()
    ChangeHappen = 1
End Sub

Private Sub txtComments_AfterUpdate()
    ChangeHappen = 1
End Sub
```

```vba
Private Sub txtCoName_AfterUpdate()
    ChangeHappen = 1
End Sub


Private Sub txtCoPhone_AfterUpdate()
    ChangeHappen = 1
End Sub


Private Sub txtCoState_AfterUpdate()
    ChangeHappen = 1
End Sub


Private Sub txtCoWebsite_AfterUpdate()
    ChangeHappen = 1
End Sub


Private Sub txtCoZip_AfterUpdate()
    ChangeHappen = 1
End Sub


'The following code is referred to more than once throughout other code
'within this project.


Private Sub LoadData(RowNumber As Long)
    On Error GoTo Oops_Error


    Dim ws As Worksheet
    Dim iRowCount As Integer

    Set ws = ActiveSheet
    frmVendor.txtRowNo.Value = RowNumber

    With Range("rngVendorInfo")
        iRowCount = .Rows.Count

        Me.txtTotalRecords = iRowCount - 1
        Me.txtRecordNo = RowNumber - 1

    End With

    Exit Sub

    'Displays a message if an error occurs.
Oops_Error:
    MsgBox Err.Number & " " & Err.Description

End Sub


Public Sub GetRecords()
    On Error GoTo Oops_Error

    vaInfo = rngData.Value

    txtVendorID.Value = vaInfo(1, 1)
    txtDateEntered.Value = vaInfo(1, 5)
    cboStatus.Value = vaInfo(1, 6)
```

```vba
        txtCoName.Value = vaInfo(1, 7)
        txtCoAddress.Value = vaInfo(1, 8)
        txtCoCity.Value = vaInfo(1, 9)
        txtCoState.Value = vaInfo(1, 10)
        txtCoZip.Value = vaInfo(1, 11)
        txtCoPhone.Value = vaInfo(1, 12)
        txtCoEmail.Value = vaInfo(1, 13)
        txtCoWebsite.Value = vaInfo(1, 14)
        txtComments.Value = vaInfo(1, 15)

    Exit Sub

    'Displays a message if an error occurs.
Oops_Error:
    MsgBox Err.Number & " " & Err.Description

End Sub



Public Sub NavRec()
    On Error GoTo Oops_Error


    frmVendor.lblRecOfRec.Caption = frmVendor.txtRecordNo.Value & "  of  " &
frmVendor.txtTotalRecords.Value
    Exit Sub

    'Displays a message if an error occurs.
Oops_Error:
    MsgBox Err.Number & " " & Err.Description

End Sub



Private Sub NewLoadData(RowNumber As Long)
    On Error GoTo Oops_Error

    frmVendor.txtRowNo.Value = Me.txtRowNo

    Dim iRowCount As Integer

    With Range("rngVendorInfo")
        iRowCount = .Rows.Count
        Me.txtTotalRecords = iRowCount - 1
        Me.txtRecordNo = RowNumber - 1

    End With

    Exit Sub

    'Displays a message if an error occurs.
Oops_Error:
    MsgBox Err.Number & " " & Err.Description

End Sub



Public Sub RecordFound()
    On Error GoTo Oops_Error

    FndInfo = fnddata.Value

    txtVendorID.Value = FndInfo(1, 1)
    txtDateEntered.Value = FndInfo(1, 5)
```

```
        cboStatus.Value = FndInfo(1, 6)
        txtCoName.Value = FndInfo(1, 7)
        txtCoAddress.Value = FndInfo(1, 8)
        txtCoCity.Value = FndInfo(1, 9)
        txtCoState.Value = FndInfo(1, 10)
        txtCoZip.Value = FndInfo(1, 11)
        txtCoPhone.Value = FndInfo(1, 12)
        txtCoEmail.Value = FndInfo(1, 13)
        txtCoWebsite.Value = FndInfo(1, 14)
        txtComments.Value = FndInfo(1, 15)

    Exit Sub

    'Displays a message if an error occurs.
Oops_Error:
    MsgBox Err.Number & " " & Err.Description

End Sub


Public Sub DisableObjects()
    On Error GoTo Oops_Error

    'Locks all Text Box fields on the form if the cbostatus object
    'is set to closed.
    Dim cNewTxtCont As Control

    For Each cNewTxtCont In Me.Controls
        If TypeName(cNewTxtCont) = "TextBox" And Me.cboStatus.Value = "Closed" And
cNewTxtCont.Name <> "txtFindVendorID" Then
            cNewTxtCont.Locked = True

        Else
            If TypeName(cNewTxtCont) = "TextBox" And Me.cboStatus.Value = "Active" Then
                txtVendorID.Locked = True
                txtDateEntered.Locked = True
                cNewTxtCont.Locked = False

            End If
        End If

    Next cNewTxtCont

    Exit Sub

    'Displays a message if an error occurs.
Oops_Error:
    MsgBox Err.Number & " " & Err.Description

End Sub


Public Sub AddToWorkbook()
    On Error GoTo Oops_Error

    Call UpdateChanges

    Worksheets("VendorData").Select
    NewLoadData frmVendor.txtRowNo.Value

    With Range("rngVendorInfo")
        Set UCdata = Range("rngVendorInfo").Rows(txtRowNo)
        UCdata.Value = UCInfo
    End With

        Exit Sub
```

[handwritten annotation: "Did Not Write to frmConnection" with a checkmark]

```
        'Displays a message if an error occurs.
Oops_Error:
        MsgBox Err.Number & " " & Err.Description

End Sub



Public Sub UpdateChanges()
    On Error GoTo Oops_Error

    UCInfo(1) = txtVendorID.Value
    UCInfo(2) = WhoAreYou
    UCInfo(3) = Date
    UCInfo(4) = Time
    UCInfo(5) = txtDateEntered.Value
    UCInfo(6) = cboStatus.Value
    UCInfo(7) = txtCoName.Value
    UCInfo(8) = txtCoAddress.Value
    UCInfo(9) = txtCoCity.Value
    UCInfo(10) = txtCoState.Value
    UCInfo(11) = txtCoZip.Value
    UCInfo(12) = txtCoPhone.Value
    UCInfo(13) = txtCoEmail.Value
    UCInfo(14) = txtCoWebsite.Value
    UCInfo(15) = txtComments.Value


    Exit Sub

    'Displays a message if an error occurs.
Oops_Error:
    MsgBox "Problem is here." & Err.Number & " " & Err.Description

End Sub

Public Sub CheckForChange()
'Ensures, if a user makes a change to the data in a field and forgets to click
'on the Update button a warning dialog box appears.

    If ChangeHappen = "1" Then

        Dim strAnswer As String
        strAnswer = MsgBox("You have made a change to this record. Do you wish to update
the record?", vbQuestion + vbYesNo, "Update record?")

        'If the user selects "Yes" then update.
        If strAnswer = vbYes Then
            ChangeHappen = 0
            Call UpdateChanges

            'Update the Workbook with the newly modified data.
            With Range("rngVendorInfo")
                Set UCdata = Range("rngVendorInfo").Rows(txtRowNo)
                UCdata.Value = UCInfo
            End With

        Else
            ChangeHappen = 0
        End If

    End If
End Sub
```

```vba
Public Function WhoAreYou() As String
    WhoAreYou = Environ("USERNAME")
End Function


Public Sub GenUniqueNum()
    On Error GoTo Oops_Error

    'Select the worksheet with the list of data.
    Sheets("VendorData").Select

    'Look at the column with the Vendor ID information.
    Dim oRg As Range, iMax As Variant, mxVal As Integer
    Set oRg = Worksheets("VendorData").Range("rngVendorID")

    'Find the maximum Vendor ID.
    iMax = Application.Max(oRg)
    mxVal = iMax

    'Assign the maximum Vendor ID to a variable.  Then select the worksheet you
    'will paste the variable value.
    Dim NewVendorID As Integer
    NewVendorID = mxVal
    Worksheets("Admin").Select

    'Place Max Value of Vendor ID range in this cell.  Although not needed, it helps
    'visually when testing.
    Worksheets("Admin").Range("C2") = NewVendorID
    Worksheets("Admin").Range("E2") = NewVendorID + 1

    Exit Sub

    'Displays a message if an error occurs.
Oops_Error:
    MsgBox Err.Number & " " & Err.Description

End Sub
```

Final Steps

1. After entering the code, remember to select Save from the menu bar.

2. Now that the project is completed, you are ready to begin testing the User Form. To assist you with testing, refer to Step Six: How to Use the User Form. It will explain what to expect when working with the User Form.

3. Verify the User Form is selected, prior to running the code.

4. Remember, to run your code, press the [F5] key or select Run Sub/UserForm on the toolbar in the VBE window.

Prior to Deployment

Thoroughly test your User Form. If you have any issues, make corrections and retest as necessary, until your User Form is working properly. If for any reason you are having an issue, start at the beginning and review each line of code, line by line. The most common issue will usually result from extra spaces or misspelled words. Starting back at the beginning of this chapter will help you determine if you overlooked anything. Also, verify that your code reference matches the name of the object.

EXAMPLE

The property name for the printer object is imgPrintRecordBtn. Therefore the Click subroutine code should include this name reference as follows.

```
Private Sub imgPrintRecordBtn_Click()
```

If these two names do not match, you will receive an error message.

NOTE   Keep in mind, if you commented out the "ThisWorkbook" code referenced in the "This Workbook Code" section as was recommended, remember to uncomment it prior to moving to the next step. Save and retest your User Form one final time.

Step Five: Deploy User Form

Now that your project is completed you are ready to make it accessible to the user. To do this, you will create a shortcut on the users desktop.

1. Locate and right-click on the Vendor Management.xls workbook you created.

2. From the shortcut menu select Send To and Desktop (create shortcut). This will place a new shortcut onto your desktop. Remember, you can save your shortcut to any folder. However, the desktop is the most easily accessible area. The choice is yours.

3. You can accept the generic shortcut default icon or right-click on the shortcut icon and select Properties.

4. Click on Change Icon… on the Shortcut tab. Choose a new icon.

5. To start using the new User Form, double click on the new Shortcut icon.

Helpful Tips

If you are experiencing any issues with your new User Form, first and foremost, refer back to the beginning of this Chapter and compare the code you entered to what is in the book. Make sure everything has been entered in correctly and your objects on the User Form are also named correctly. This usually will resolve most of your common issues.

However, although not required, it is highly recommended you close out of Excel prior to opening up the Vendor User Form.

If clicking the icon does not open the Vendor User Form check the following.

1. Is Excel already open?
   - If Excel was improperly closed previously, there is the possibility Excel is still running in the background. Open the Task Manager List dialog box by pressing the [Ctrl], [Alt] and the [Delete] keys simultaneously.
   - Then select the Processes tab. Click on the Image Name column header to sort the list information.
   - Locate and select Excel.EXE and then press the End Process button.
   - Then when the Task Manager Warning dialog box appears, select the Yes button.
   - Try to open the Vendor User Form, again.

2. Verify there are no other opened dialog boxes. If so, close out of them and then try again.

To view other helpful tips, tutorials and snippets of code, we encourage you to visit our website at: http://www.richardsjournals.com

Step Six: How to Use the User Form

A User Form can be designed to automatically open when a user double-clicks on a workbook shortcut icon; via a link; by pressing keyboard shortcuts, or as the result of clicking a button. The option is dependent upon the purpose of the User Form or it could be just a matter of preference.

To help maintain the integrity of the data captured from the User Form, most well designed User Forms hide the Excel workbook when opened. This design approach amazes people, because many find it hard to believe an Excel workbook can work this way. For this reason, User Forms are extremely popular with people who are not very comfortable working with an Excel workbook.

Managing the Workbook Data with the User Form

An Excel workbook designed to capture data usually consists of field names stored in a columnar header format in row 1 of a Worksheet. Each row of information stored is then considered a record. This type of approach permits you to treat a workbook as a data repository.

In this example, the User Form permits you to use a previous and next button to navigate between the records in the workbook. The record locator above the navigation buttons displays the record the user is currently viewing from the total records stored within the workbook.

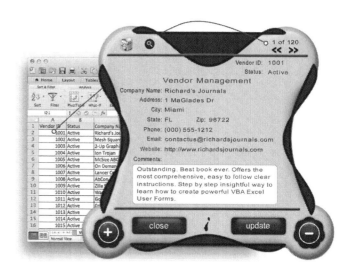

Add New Record Button

The data maintained in the workbook is stored in a list and each newly added record is placed at the bottom of that list. Clicking the plus button located in the lower left corner of the form permits a user to add a new record.

The following changes will occur after clicking the Add New Record (+) button:

- The User Form displays a blank record.

- The close button changes to a cancel button.

- The update button changes to a save button.

- The add new record or + button is hidden.

- The delete current record or - button is hidden.

- The record of record display is hidden.

- The previous and next navigation buttons are hidden.

- A new Vendor ID will be automatically generated.

- The Status field will default to Active.

- Disable the search button.

- Disable the print button.

It is only possible to manipulate these items on the User Form because each image was added to the User Form separately during the design phase. Through the use of code, you're able to hide and display each individual item based on specific user interactions with the User Form.

Hiding the individual items is a choice. Other methods such as disabling the images or displaying message boxes could have been just as effective. It all comes down to how you choose to manage the User Form environment based on the user's interaction with the User Form.

Cancel Button

When the User Form is open the Cancel button is hidden by default. It will display when you click on the

 Add New Record button. Selecting the Cancel button displays a Yes or No prompt.

"Are you sure you want to cancel this entry?"

- Selecting the Yes button when the warning message window appears will undo the new entry and then returns the user back to the current records.

- Selecting the No button when the warning message window appears will keep the user on the same page and the entries will remain in tact.

Update Button

 Selecting the Update button saves all recent entries.

Save Button

 When the User Form is open the Save button is hidden by default. It will display when you click on the Add New Record button. Clicking the Save button after entering a new record adds the new entry to the workbook list of records.

Close Button

 Selecting the Close button closes the User Form and saves all recent entries.

Delete Current Record Button

 Clicking the minus button located in the lower right corner of the form permits a user to delete the current record from the list on the workbook.

The User Form will display the following warning yes or no message after clicking the Delete Current Record (-) button:

"Are you sure you want to delete this record?"

- Selecting the Yes button when the warning message window appears deletes the current record from list of records on the workbook.

- Selecting the No button when the warning message window appears allows the record to remain in the list on the workbook.

Warning Message Window

A warning message window will appear when the user selects either the Cancel or Delete buttons.

Search Button

 Clicking the search icon, located in the upper left corner of the form next to the printer icon, displays the search toolbar and permits the user to search the workbook for a specific record based on the entered Vendor ID number.

A message displays to notify the user when the entered Vendor ID number is not located. If the entered number is located, the record displays. Clicking the search icon again hides the search toolbar.

Send an E-mail

Double-clicking an e-mail address in the E-mail field automatically opens Outlook. The To field populates with the current e-mail address identified in the E-mail field.

Open a Web Page

Double-clicking the URL referenced in the Website field automatically opens the referenced Web Page.

Print the Current Record

Clicking the printer icon in the upper left corner of the form prints the current record.

View Help Document

 Clicking the help icon located at the bottom of the User Form opens the User Guide Microsoft Word document. The document that displays is a frequently asked questions sheet for the user.

Appendix:
Project
Checklist

Project Overview Checklist

☐ Purpose of the User Form

There is a need for a user-friendly application to store, retrieve and update all Vendor company information.

☐ Create the Folder Structure

Create a folder on your Desktop titled Vendor Data. Then create subfolders titled Code Snippets, Documents, Forms and Images.

☐ Identify Objects

Create a list of all objects you anticipate you will need on your User Form.

Fields (UserForm / Worksheet)
- ✓ Vendor ID
- ✓ Last Modify By
- ✓ Date Modified
- ✓ Time Modified
- ✓ Date of Entry
- ✓ Status
- ✓ Company Name
- ✓ Address
- ✓ City
- ✓ State
- ✓ Zip
- ✓ Phone
- ✓ Email
- ✓ Website
- ✓ Comments
- ✓ * Status Options
- ✓ * Last Used Vendor ID

Image used as buttons

Transparent Images
- ✓ Print
- ✓ Open/Close Search Toolbar
- ✓ Info
- ✓ Search

Opaque (Regular) Images
- ✓ Previous
- ✓ Next
- ✓ Add Record
- ✓ Close
- ✓ Cancel
- ✓ Update
- ✓ Save
- ✓ Delete Record

** UserForm Hidden Fields
- ✓ Record Number
- ✓ Total Records
- ✓ Next Vendor ID Number
- ✓ Row Number
- ✓ Find Vendor ID
- ✓ Set Focus

* Located on the Admin tab in the Workbook and also referenced within the code.

** These fields will be hidden on the UserForm and the captured data will be referenced within the code.

☐ **Create a Rough Sketch**

Create a rough sketch of the User Form based on the objects you have identified.

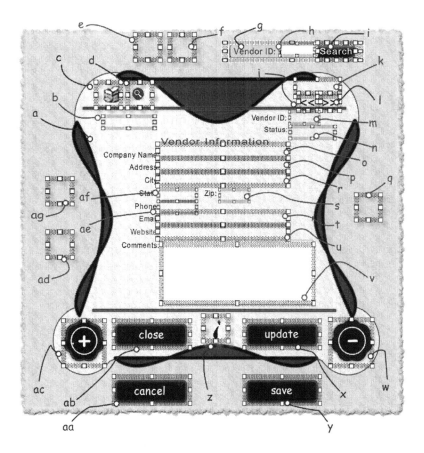

a. Image: imgBackground
b. Text Box: txtDateEntered
c. Image: imgPrintRecordBtn
d. Image: imgOpenToolbarBtn
e. Text Box: txtRecordNo
f. Text Box: txtTotalRecords
g. Image: imgSearchToolbar
h. Text Box: txtFindVendorID
i. Image: imgSearchBtn
j. Image: imgPrevRecordBtn
k. Label Box: lblRecOfRec
l. Image: imgNextRecordBtn
m. Text Box: txtVendorID
n. Combo Box: cboStatus
o. Text Box: txtCoName
p. Text Box: txtCoAddress
q. Text Box: txtFocusHere
r. Text Box: txtCoCity
s. Text Box: txtCoZip
t. Text Box: txtCoEmail
u. Text Box: txtCoWebsite
v. Text Box: txtComments
w. Image: imgDeleteRecordBtn

x. Image: imgUpdateBtn
y. Image: imgSaveBtn
z. Image: imgInfoBtn
aa. Image: imgCancelBtn
ab. Image: imgCloseFormBtn
ac. Image: imgAddRecordBtn
ad. Text Box: txtNextVendorID
ae. Text Box: txtCoPhone
af. Text Box: txtCoState
ag. Text Box: txtRowNo

☐ Identify User Form Images

Identify the images you will need to create for you User Form.

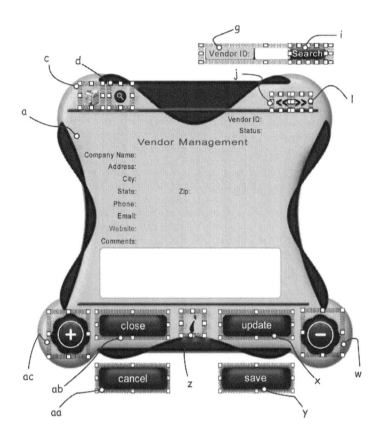

Image Names and Descriptions

Through the use of code all of the images referenced in the following tables except the background image will be converted to a button.

	Property Name	Object Type	Picture	Description
☐ a.	imgBackground	Image	Background.jpg	This image will be the used as the background image for the User Form.
☐ c.	imgPrintRecordBtn	Image (Transparent)	None	Prints the current viewable record and User Form.
☐ d.	imgOpenToolbarBtn	Image (Transparent)	None	Opens or hides the Search Toolbar.

	Property Name	Object Type	Picture	Description
☐ g.	imgSearchToolbar	Image	SearchToolbar.jpg	The search toolbar will appear or close when the Open Search Toolbar button is selected.
				Used to search the User Form based on Vendor ID.
☐ i.	imgSearchBtn	Image (Transparent)	None	Clicking the Search Button will search the User Form for the Vendor ID number entered into the Search Toolbar field.
				If the Vendor ID entered is valid the User Form will display the record.
				Regardless if the search is successful or not the the criteria search field on the Search Toolbar will be cleared.
				If the Vendor ID can not be located, the message [Vendor ID] is not a valid Vendor ID number. Please try again."
				If the search field is blank then the user will receive the message, "Please enter a Vendor ID number."
☐ j.	imgPrevRecordBtn	Image	PrevRecordBtn.jpg	Navigates to the previous record. If there are changes to the current record, prompt the user to accept or cancel changes.
☐ i.	imgNextRecordBtn	Image	NextRecordBtn.jpg	Navigates to the next record. If there are changes to the current record, prompt the user to accept or cancel changes.
☐ w.	imgDeleteRecordBtn	Image	DeleteRecordBtn.jpg	Prior to deleting the current record the user will receive a message prompt, "Are you sure you want to delete this record?" along with a "Yes" and "No" button option.
☐ x.	imgUpdateBtn	Image	UpdateBtn.jpg	Any changes to the data will be saved.
☐ y.	imgSaveBtn	Image	SaveBtn.jpg	This button only appears when the Add Record Button is selected.
				Selecting Save button displays a message box "New record has been saved." .
				Returns to the User Form to view records.
				Hides the Cancel and Save button.
				Displays the Record of Record label, the Add Record button, the Close button, the Update button, the Previous Record button, the Next Record button, and the Delete Record button.
☐ z.	imgInfoBtn	Image (Transparent)	None	Opens a User Guide document.
☐ aa.	imgCancelBtn	Image	CancelBtn.jpg	This button only appears when the Add Record Button is selected.
				Returns to the User Form to view records.
				Will undo any data entry entered after the Add Record Button was selected.
				Hides the Save button.
				Displays the Record of Record label, the Add Record button, the Close button, the Update button, the Previous Record button, the Next Record button, and the Delete Record button.

Item	Name	Type	Image Name	Description
☐ ab.	imgCloseFormBtn	Image	CloseFormBtn.jpg	A message prompt displays, "Are you sure you want to close this User Form?" along with a "Yes" and "No" button option.
☐ ac.	imgAddRecordBtn	Image	AddRecordBtn.jpg	Select to add a new record. When the button is selected the Record of Record label, the Add Record button, the Close button, the Update button, the Previous Record button, the Next Record button, and the Delete Record button will be automatically hidden. The Cancel and Save button will appear.

☐ Identify User Form Objects Combo Box, Label and Text Boxes

The following Text Boxes, Label and Combo Boxes have been identified during the planning phase and should be used as a guide during the development process.

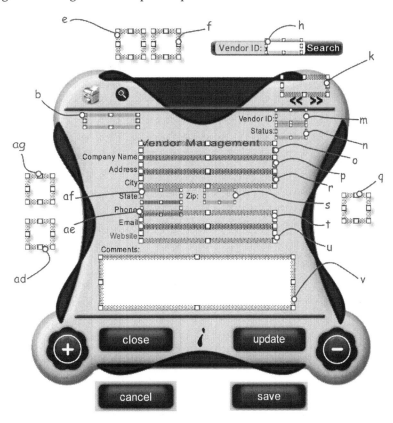

Label, Combo Box, and Text Box Names and Descriptions

Item	Name	Type	Property Name	Description
☐ b.	Date Entered	Text Box (Hidden)	txtRecordNo	This is the position of the record in the data range.
☐ e.	Record Number	Text Box (Hidden)	txtRecordNo	This is the position of the record in the data range.
☐ f.	Total Records	Text Box (Hidden)	txtTotalRecords	This is the total number of records in the data range.

Item	Name	Type	Property Name	Description
☐ h.	Find Vendor ID	Text Box	txtFindVendorID	Used to search the User Form based on Vendor ID. The Search Criteria field is located on the Search Toolbar and will accept only a maximum of four numbers. The restriction to only four numbers is based on the maximum characters in a Vendor ID. Only numbers are accepted in this field.
☐ k.	Record of Records	Label	lblRecOfRec	Displays the position of the current record in the total number of records. (Record number of Total Records)
☐ m.	Vendor ID	Text Box	txtVendorID	Automatically populates with the txtNextVendorID number when a new record is added.
☐ n.	Status	Combo Box	cboStatus	Drop down list displays status choices.
☐ o.	Company Name	Text Box	txtCoName	Enter the Vendor's Name.
☐ p.	Company Address	Text Box	txtCoAddress	Enter the Vendor's address.
☐ q.	Focus Here	Text Box	txtFocusHere	Set's the focus of the cursor to this field. Helps to establish if a change was made to a field and prevents the user from accidently modifying a field when navigating between records.
☐ r.	Company City	Text Box	txtCoCity	Enter the Vendor's city of residence.
☐ s.	Company Zip	Text Box	txtCoZip	Enter the Vendor's Zip code.
☐ t.	Company E-mail	Text Box	txtCoEmail	Enter the Vendor's e-mail address. Double clicking this field will open an e-mail and automatically populate the To, Subject and Body of the e-mail with information from the fields on the User Form.
☐ u.	Company Website	Text Box	txtCoWebsite	Enter the Vendor's website. Double clicking this field will automatically open the Vendor's website as referenced in the field.
☐ v.	Comments	Text Box	txtComments	Enter any comments related to the Vendor. Displays multiple lines of information.
☐ ad.	Next Vendor ID	Text Box (Hidden)	txtNextVendorID	This field will automatically populate with the next available Vendor ID number.
☐ ae.	Company Phone Number	Text Box	txtCoPhone	Enter the Vendor's phone number. As the phone number the field automatically displays parenthesis and a hyphen. Although the User Form will display the phone number with parenthesis and a hyphen the phone number entered into this field will be stored with the numbers only in the workbook. Example: (000)555-1212 will be stored as 0005551212 in the workbook. Data entry restricted to only numbers.
☐ af.	Company State	Text Box	txtCoState	Enter the Vendor's state of residence.
☐ ag.	Row Number	Text Box (Hidden)	txtRowNo	Displays the row number in the workbook of the current record.

Workbook Specifications

☐ Save workbook as "Vendor Management.xls".

☐ Based on coding the workbook should be hidden from view.

☐ The workbook data should only be accessible through the VBA User Form.

Worksheet Specifications

Create two worksheets.

☐ **VendorData** This will house all of the Vendor information entered into the VBA User Form.

☐ **Admin** This will contain information related to the Status drop down list, and Vendor. This worksheet will be hidden.

Add Test Data

☐ Create the following Column headers and enter the Test data on the VendorData worksheet. Cells C2, D2 and E2 have been intentionally left blank. These cells will be populated after you begin using the User Form.

Column(s)	Column Header
A1	Vendor ID
B1	Last Modify By
C1	Date Modified
D1	Time Modified
E1	Date of Entry
F1	Status
G1	Company Name
H1	Address
I1	City
J1	State
K1	Zip
L1	Phone
M1	E-mail

Column(s)	Data
A2	1001
B2	AD23112
C2	
D2	
E2	
F2	Active
G2	Richard's Journals
H2	1 MaGlades dr
I2	Miami
J2	FL
K2	96722
L2	0005551212
M2	contactus@richardsjournals.com

N1	Website
O1	Comments

N2	http://www.richardsjournals.com
O2	Specializes in high quality books.

☐ Create the following Column headers and enter the Test data on the Admin worksheet.

Column(s)	Column Header
A1	Status Options
C1	Last Vendor ID

Column(s)	Data
A1	Active
A2	Closed
C2	1001

Ranges

Create four ranges using the Define Name range method.

☐ rngVendorID   =OFFSET(VendorData!$A$1,0,0,COUNTA(VendorData!$A:$A),1)

☐ rngVendorInfo   =OFFSET(VendorData!$A$1,0,0,COUNTA(VendorData!$A:$A),15)

☐ rngStatus   =OFFSET(Admin!$A$1,0,0,COUNTA(Admin!$A:$A),1)

☐ rngVendorInfoTmp   Create range through the use of code.

Coding Requirements

☐ **User Form**

- Automatically hide the Excel workbook and display only the User Form.

- Automatically set the Font, Font Style and size for all Text Boxes on the User Form.

- Automatically populate the User Form with data from the Workbook.

- Track changes to User Form.

- When opening the User Form set the cursors focus to a generic field to prevent the user from accidental altering a field's data.

☐ **Print Button**

- Clicking the Print button will automatically print the current record and User Form.

☐   **Open Search Toolbar**

- Clicking the Open Search button will cause the Search Toolbar to open or close.

- The Search Toolbar consists of a Search Criteria field and the Search Button.

☐   **Search Criteria field**

- This field is located on the Search Toolbar.

- A Vendor ID is needed to complete the search.

- Restrict this field to only four numbers.

☐   **Search Button**

- Clicking this button will search for the Vendor ID number entered on the Search Toolbar.

- If the Vendor ID entered is valid the User Form will display the record.

- Regardless if the search is successful or not the criteria search field on the Search Toolbar will be cleared.

- If the Vendor ID cannot be located, the message "[Vendor ID number] is not a valid Vendor ID number. Please try again."

- If the search field is blank then the user will receive the message, "Please enter a Vendor ID number."

☐   **Vendor ID**

- Automatically generate a unique Vendor ID.

☐   **Previous Record Button**

- Permits the user to navigate to the previous record.

- Display a message notifying the user they are on the first record.

- If the data is modified, a message will display, "You have made a change to this record. Do you wish to update the record?"

☐   **Next Record Button**

- Permits the user to navigate to the next record.

- Display a message notifying the user they are on the last record.

- If the data is modified, a message will display, "You have made a change to this record. Do you wish to update the record?"

☐   **Status**

- Drop down list is set to the rngStatus range on the Admin page.

- Locks down all fields for a record when the status is changed to a "Closed" status.

☐ **Add Record Button**

- Allows the user to add a new record to the workbook.

- When the user clicks on this button the Record of Record label, the Add Record button, Close button, Update button, Delete button, Previous and Next Record navigation buttons will be automatically hidden.

- When the user clicks on this button the Cancel and Save button will automatically appear in the same location as the Close and Update button.

☐ **Close User Form button**

- Prior to closing the User Form all changes to the data will be saved and the user will receive a message prompt.

☐ **Update button**

- This will save any changes made to the current record.

☐ **Cancel button**

- This button is visible only when the user clicks on the Add Record Button.

- After it is clicked the user will return to the User Form to view the records.

- This will undo all entries on the New Record since the Add Record Button was selected.

- The Save button will automatically be hidden when the user clicks on this button.

- When the user clicks on this button the Record of Record label, the Add Record button, Close button, Update button, Delete button, Previous and Next Record navigation buttons will automatically display.

☐ **Save Button**

- This button will only appear when the user clicks on the Add Record Button.

- Clicking the Save button will display a message box "New record has been saved."

- Returns the user back to the User Form to view records.

- Hides the Cancel and Save button.

- Displays the Record of Record label, Add Record button, Close button, Update button, Previous Record, Next Record, and the Delete Record buttons.

☐ **Delete Current Record Button**

- Prior to deleting the current record the user will receive a message prompt, "Are you sure you want to delete this record?" along with a "Yes" and "No" button option.

☐ **Vendor's E-mail**

- Double clicking this field will open an e-mail User Form and automatically populate the To, Subject and Body of the e-mail with information from the fields on the current User Form.

☐ **Vendor's Website**

- Double clicking this field will automatically open the Vendor's website as referenced in the field.

☐ **Vendor's Phone Number**

- As the user enters the Vendor's phone number the field will automatically display the parenthesis around the area code and the hyphen.

- Store the phone number in the workbook as numbers only with no parenthesis or hyphen.

- Restrict this field to numbers only.

☐ **Comments**

- Display multiple lines of data.

- If the data entered exceeds the field height then add a vertical scroll bar.

Folder Structure

Create the following folder structure to house all of the items related to the Vendor User Form. The project Excel workbook will be stored under the main folder "Vendor Project".

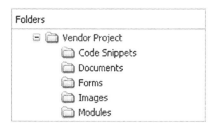

☐	**Vendor Project**	Store the Vendor Management.xls workbook.
☐	**Code Snippets**	Store all code snippets gathered during your research and development phase.
☐	**Documents**	Used to maintain project notes and Word templates.
☐	**Forms**	Backup all finalized User Forms.
☐	**Images**	Store all images associated with the User Form in this folder.
☐	**Modules**	Backup all modules associated with the User Form in this folder.

Create Shortcut

To make the User Form easily accessible create a shortcut for the Vendor Management.xls workbook on your Desktop. At this point you can choose to assign your own unique icon to the shortcut.

Appendix:
User Form
Guide

Vendor Management User Form

Guide
Version 1.0

Created by
Richard Brooks

Table of Contents

Purpose

This document provides a user with a brief overview of all the current attributes of the Vendor User Form features.

Resources

Name	Role
John Doe Department: Inventory Management Phone: (000) 555-1213 E-mail: john.doe@abc00.com	Owner
Richard Brooks Department: Database Engineering Dept. Phone: (000) 555-1212 E-mail: contactus@richardsjournals.com	Developer

Documentation

The document includes an overview of the existing features within the Vendor Management User Form Guide.

Revision	Document Title	Date
Version 1.0	Vendor Management User Form Guide.doc	

Corrections or comments

If you have corrections or comments about this document, please contact:

Richard Brooks
Department: Database Engineering Dept.
Phone: (000) 555-1212
E-mail: contactus@richardsjournals.com

Database Design

The Vendor Management User Form has been designed using the Microsoft Excel application. The User Form is separated into two parts described as the front end and back end. The back end of the User Form consists of the workbook that will maintain the data captured from the User Form. The front end of the User Form is the Graphical Interface people will user to enter their data.

Basic Workflow

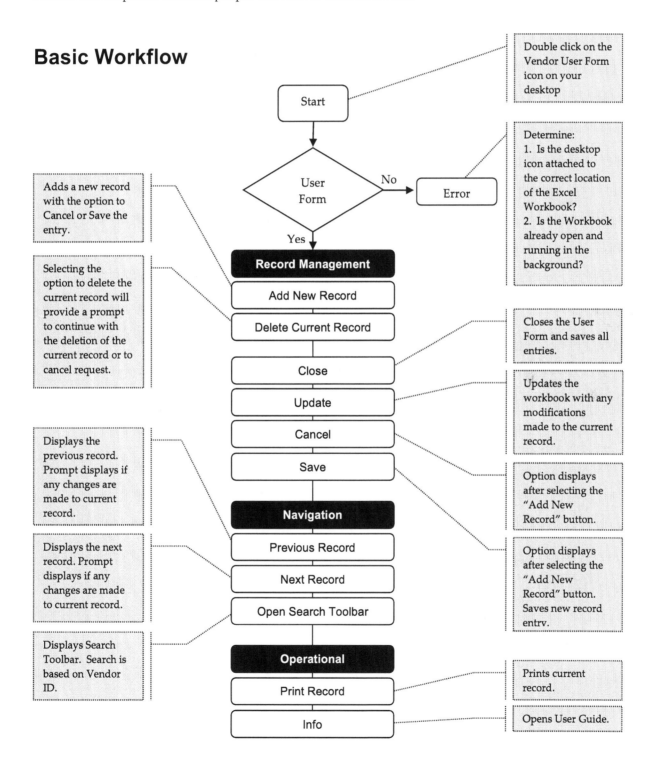

Open the User Form

Although not required, it is highly recommended you close out of Excel prior to opening up the Vendor User Form. To open the Vendor User Form, double click on the shortcut icon on the desktop. By default the User Form will display the last record in the User Form.

If clicking the icon does not open the Vendor User Form check the following.

3. Is Excel already open?
    - If Excel was improperly closed previously, there is the possibility Excel is still running in the background. Open the Task List dialog box by pressing the [Ctrl], [Alt] and the [Delete] keys simultaneously.
    - Then select the Processes tab. Click on the Image Name column header to sort the list information.
    - Locate and select Excel.EXE and then press the End Process button.
    - Then when the Task Manager Warning dialog box appears, select the Yes button.
    - Try to open the Vendor User Form, again.

4. Verify there are no other opened dialog boxes. If so, close out of them and then try again.

Built In Features

Click into any one of the fields to enter your data. To advance to the next field you can press the Tab key on your keyboard.

- When entering phone number the parenthesis will automatically populate within the field.
- Double clicking an E-mail address in the E-mail field will open up Microsoft Outlook.
- Double clicking the URL in the Website field will automatically open up the website.
- The Vendor ID is auto generated and will increase incrementally when you add a new record.
- The Status field will display a drop down list when selected.
- To view the User Guide document at anytime you can select the Info icon located at the bottom of the User Form.
- Click on the plus button to add a new record or the minus button to delete the current record.
- Closing the User Form will automatically save the information you entered into the User Form.
- Clicking the Search icon will permit you to Search the User Form for a specific record based on the entered Vendor ID.
- Selecting the Printer icon will print the current record.
- If you are attempting to navigate to the next or previous record a prompt will appear, if you do not select the Update button after making changes to the current record.

18551755R00086

Made in the USA
Lexington, KY
11 November 2012